THE PRODIGAL WOW

A LONG LOST FRIEND RETURNS

JOHANN GEORG HOHMAN

WITH AN INTRODUCTION & COMMENTARY BY

DENNIS LOGAN

THE PRODIGAL

Wow A Long Lost Friend Returns
With an Introduction & Commentary by **Dennis Logan**

This edition contains:

1. A restored facsimile reproduction of the 1820 text.
2. A modernized typeset edition for clarity and readability.
3. A 2025 commentary and expansion grounded in Christian devotional folk practice.

The historical material in this book is presented for its cultural and archival value.
Penemue Media does not endorse any outdated medical, topical, or physical remedies contained in the 19th-century text.
For any health-related matter, consult qualified medical professionals.

Scriptural quotations, where used, are from public-domain translations.

Published by Penemue Media, LLC
Richmond, Virginia

Interior design, restoration, and commentary by Dennis Logan.

ISBN: 978-1-964297-18-7

Printed in the United States of America.
First Penemue Media Edition: 2025

EDITORIAL PREFACE

This volume presents **three complete forms** of *The Long Lost Friend*:

1. the original **facsimile**,
2. a **modernized typeset** for clarity, and
3. a **2025 expansion** building upon its historical tradition.

The original text, written in 1820, includes medical remedies, household recipes, and folk cures that were common in rural America but are **not medically safe** or appropriate for modern use. Such passages are preserved only for their historical value.
We do not endorse any medical or topical application contained in the 19th-century material.
For any emergency or condition requiring treatment, **consult qualified medical professionals**.

The purpose of this edition is not to revive outdated practices, but to **preserve the historical record**, offer a **readable modern rendering**, and present an **honest continuation** of the Christian folk-magic tradition that shaped early American life. The new material is grounded in scripture, verifiable Braucherei tradition, and centuries of Christian devotional practice. Nothing has been added that departs from the spiritual lineage of the original.

This book is offered for study, devotion, and heritage—
not for unsupervised experimentation.
May it be read with wisdom, reverence, and discernment.

— **Penemue Media, 2025**

A Word on Cultural Respect and Honest Naming

This edition approaches the history of *The Long Lost Friend* with care. Although the book was later reissued as **"Pow-Wows; or, The Long Lost Friend,"** we acknowledge openly that this title was a product of misunderstanding and sensationalism, not of historical truth.

The Pennsylvania German tradition upon which Hohman drew is properly called **Braucherei**, often translated simply as "the practice" or "the work." It is a form of Christian folk-healing rooted in:

- scripture,
- Psalms,
- spoken blessings,
- simple gestures,
- and the daily devotional life of rural families.

It has **no connection** to Native American powwow ceremonies, which are culturally sacred and carry their own heritage, meaning, and spiritual authority.

By restoring this clarity, we honor both traditions:

- **Native American ceremonies**, which deserve respect and accurate representation, and
- **Braucherei**, which deserves to be understood on its own terms and within its own lineage.

This edition preserves that integrity.

DEDICATION

To all who seek peace in troubled times,
and to every household that has whispered a prayer
over the sick, the weary, the fearful, and the uncertain.

To the quiet believers who never asked for recognition
but who kept faith alive in kitchens, fields, workshops,
and bedrooms lit by a single lamp.

To the ones who have carried blessings forward
from one generation to the next,
that the light might not be lost.

And to the reader—
may this old friend stand beside you
with strength, gentleness, and grace.

Introduction:
A New Friend for a New Time

When *The Long Lost Friend* first stepped into the world in 1820, the United States was a young nation still finding its shape and soul. The War of 1812 had ended only a few years earlier, and the identity of "America" itself was still under negotiation. The Industrial Revolution had not yet flooded the land with machinery; the frontier pushed westward into territories both beautiful and violent; and slavery, entrenched and defended, continued its cruelty with the full sanction of the law. It was a time of hardship, fear, uncertainty, and extraordinary resilience.

Most households lived far from doctors, courts, or any form of reliable infrastructure. A broken leg, a fever, a hostile neighbor, or a long journey could become life-or-death matters. Immigrant communities—German, Irish, African, Native, and many others—held tightly to the practices that had kept their ancestors alive. Faith mingled with folk-cure, prayer with practicality, scripture with charm. Religion did not live in pulpits alone; it lived in kitchens, barns, fields, and hearths.

It was into this world that **Johann Georg Hohman** brought his small, strange, and enduring book.

Hohman was not a theologian. He was not a physician. He was not a scholar. He was an immigrant printer who cared about the wellbeing of his community and who preserved the whispered knowledge, humble remedies, and devotional prayers that ordinary people depended on. He gathered the blessings spoken by grandmothers, the psalms recited at sickbeds, the protections used by farmers, the charms remembered from the Rhineland, and the simple, earnest Christianity of the Pennsylvania Dutch world. His goal was not fame or fortune; it was **care**.

The trustworthiness of Hohman does not come from expertise in medicine—it comes from the sincerity with which he preserved the lived spiritual and practical wisdom of his people. He wrote as one neighbor helping another. He wrote as a man who believed, wholeheartedly, that God met people in the small things. He wrote to bring peace, comfort, courage, and protection to households like his own.

Because he wrote from the heart of a living tradition,
his work did not fade.

The "Pow-Wows" Confusion and the Reissue That Changed the Book's Identity

More than eighty years after the original publication, a new generation of publishers sought to capitalize on renewed interest in folk-magic and spiritual healing. During this time, the term **"powwow"**—borrowed inaccurately from various Native American languages—had entered common speech in Pennsylvania as a colloquial term for **a folk healer**, especially among outsiders trying to describe Pennsylvania German Braucherei.

The actual powwow ceremonies of Native nations had **nothing** to do with Hohman's work.
But the word was catchy, mysterious, and marketable.

And so, in the early 20th century, publishers reissued Hohman's book under a new title:
"Pow-Wows; or, The Long Lost Friend."

Nothing inside had changed.
Only the branding had.

This created a century of misunderstanding. People believed Hohman's work was connected to Native American ceremonial practice, when in truth it was entirely German Christian folk tradition woven from scripture, hymns, Psalms, and rural Christian devotion. This edition speaks plainly about that history so that no confusion remains.

The mislabeling was not born from malice—only from an era that often blended cultures carelessly. But in 2025, we treat every tradition with the dignity and accuracy it deserves. This book acknowledges the misuse of the term "powwow," corrects the record, and returns Hohman's work to its proper lineage.

Why a Modern Continuation?

Survival is not the same as relevance.
Over two centuries have passed since Hohman published his book.
The world has changed beyond recognition.
We no longer ride wagons along forested roads or fear the collapse of a mill wheel.
We no longer treat infection with poultices or rely on charms to protect horses on night journeys.

But the human heart has not changed.

We still fear sickness.
We still worry about our children.
We still long for peace, safety, hope, and blessing.
We still face dangers—digital intrusions, identity theft, anxiety, burnout, slander through screens—that are different only in their technology. Their spiritual weight is the same.

That is why this book has not been left to die.

Some texts belong solely to their century.
This one belongs to the way ordinary people seek God in the everyday, and that need is timeless.

What This Edition Does—and Does Not Do

Our 2025 continuation does not attempt to create a new religion or import practices from outside the Christian tradition. Nor does it attempt to mimic or appropriate the ceremonies of other cultures. The new material presented here is grounded entirely in:

- scripture,
- long-standing Christian devotional practice,
- verifiable Braucherei rituals,
- and the spiritual concerns of modern people.

We add new charms only where they naturally extend the lineage Hohman left behind:

- the desire for peace at home,
- the need for protection in dangerous times,
- the hope for healing and comfort,
- and the faith that God meets His people where they are.

We do not offer superstition.
We offer continuity.

If you are reading this, you are part of that continuity. You stand in a long line of ordinary believers who sought the presence of God not only in churches but in fields, workplaces, bedrooms, kitchens, and quiet moments of worry and hope. This book stands with you as a companion—a friend to the troubled mind, the anxious heart, the weary worker, the uncertain traveler.

We revive this book not to resuscitate the dead,
but to honor the living tradition that still breathes within it.

Some books fade into silence.
Others remain companions for generations.

The Long Lost Friend has always been the latter.

May it serve you as it served those who came before you—
with faith, with gentleness, and with strength.

Before you enter these old pages,
pause for a moment and let your heart grow quiet.
These words come to you from another age—
a world of candlelight, rough-hewn tables,
winter winds through wooden boards,
neighbors helping neighbors,
and faith carried from one day to the next
by simple men and women who trusted God
with every breath and every burden.

May the peace of their world rest upon you
as you behold their words.
May you read these pages with patience,
with humility,
and with gratitude for the hands that preserved them.
May every blemish on the paper remind you
that faith does not require perfection—
only sincerity.
And may the God who watched over them
watch over you as well.

Enter now into the old friend's presence.
Let the past speak softly,
and let its blessings accompany you
as you turn each page.

THE
LONG LOST FRIEND.

OR

Faithful & Christian Instructions

CONTAINING

WONDEROUS AND WELL-TRIED

ARTS & REMEDIES,

FOR

MAN AS WELL AS ANIMALS.

WITH MANY PROOFS

Of their virtue and efficacy in healing diseases, &c. the greater part of which was never published until they appeared in print for the first time in the U. S. in the year 1820.

LITERALLY TRANSLATED FROM THE GERMAN WORK OF

JOHN GEORGE HOHMAN,

Near Reading, Alsace Township, Berks County, Penn.

HARRISBURG, PA.——1850.

PREFACE.

—

THE author should have preferred writing no preface whatever to this little book, were it not indispensably necessary, in order to meet the erroneous views some men entertain in regard to works of this character. The majority, undoubtedly, approve of the publication and sale of such books, yet some are always found who will persist in denouncing them as something wrong. This latter class I cannot help but pity for being so far led astray; and I earnestly pray every one who might find it in his power, to bring them from off their ways of error. It is true, whosoever taketh the name of Jesus in vain, committeth a great sin. Yet is it not expressly written in the 50th Psalm, according to Luther's translation: "Call upon me in the day of trouble: I will deliver thee, and thou shalt glorify me." In the Catholic translation, the same passage is found in the 49th Psalm, reading thus: "Call upon me in the day of thy trouble, and I will deliver thee, and thou shalt glorify me."

Where is the doctor who has ever banished the panting or palpitation of the heart and hideboundeness? Where is the doctor who ever banished a wheal? Where is the doctor who ever banished the mother-fits? Where is the doctor who can cure mortification when it once seizes a member of the body? All these cures, and a great many more mysterious things are contained in this book; and its author could take an oath at any time upon the fact of his having successfully applied many of the prescriptions on its pages.

I say: Any and every man who knowingly neglects using this book in saving the eye, or the leg, or any other limb of his fellow-man, is guilty of the loss of such limb, and thus committing a sin, he may forfeit to himself all hope of heaven. Such men refuse to call upon the Lord in their trouble, although he especially commands it. If men were not allowed to use sympathetic words, nor the name of the Most High, it would certainly not have been revealed to them; and what is more, the Lord would not help where they are made use of. God can in no manner be forced to intercede where it is not his divine pleasure. Another thing I have to notice here: there are men who will say, if one has used sympathetic words in vain, the medicines of doctors could not avail any, because the words did not effect a cure. This is only the excuse of physicians; because whatever cannot be cured by sympathetic words can much less be cured by any doctor's craft or cunning. I could name at any time that catholic priest whose horse was cured with mere words; and I could also give the name of the man who done it. I knew the priest well; he formerly resided in Westmoreland county. If it was desired, I could also name a reformed preacher, who cured several persons of the fever, merely by writing them some tickets for that purpose; and even the names of those persons I could mention. This preacher formerly resided in Berks county.—If men but use out of this book what they actually need, they surely commit no sin; yet wo unto those who are guilty that any one loses his life in consequence of mortification, or loses a limb, or the sight of the eye! Wo unto those who misconstrue these things at the moment of danger, or who follow the ill advise of any preacher who might teach them not to mind what the Lord says in the 50th Psalm: "Call upon me in the day of trouble: I will deliver thee, and thou shalt glorify me."—Wo unto those who in obeying the directions of a preacher, neglect using any means offered by this book against mortification, or inflammation, or the wheal. I am willing to follow the preacher in all reasonable things, yet when I am in danger and he advises me not to use any prescriptions found in this book, in such a case I shall not obey him. And wo also unto those who use the name of the Lord in vain and for trifling purposes.

I have given many proofs of the usefulness of this book, and I could yet do it at any time. I sell my books publicly, and not secretly, as other mystical works are sold. I am willing that my books should be seen by every body, and I shall not secrete or hide myself from any preacher. I, Hohman, too, have some knowledge of the scriptures, and I know when to call and pray unto the Lord for assistance. The publication of books (provided they are useful and morally right,) is not prohibited in the United States, as is the case in other countries where kings and despots hold tyrannical sway over the people. I place myself upon the broad platform of the liberty of the press and of conscience, in regard to this useful book, and it shall ever be my most heartfelt desire that all men might have an opportunity of using it to their good, in the name of Jesus.

Given at Rosenthal, near Reading, Berks county, Penn. on the 31st day of July, in the year of our Lord 1819.

JOHN GEORGE HOHMAN,
Author and original publisher of this book.

—

NOTE.

There are many in America who believe neither in a hell nor in heaven; but in Germany there are not so many of these persons found. I, Hohman, ask: Who can immediately banish the wheal, or mortification? I reply, and I, Hohman, say: All this is done by the Lord.—Therefore a hell and a heaven must exist; and I think very little of any one who dares to deny it.

TESTIMONIALS,

Which go to show at any time, that I, Hohman, have suc-cessfully applied the prescriptions of this book.

———————

Benjamin Stoudt, the son of a Lutheran school-master, at Reading, suffered dreadfully from a wheal in the eye.— In a little more than 24 hours, this eye was as sound as the other one, by the aid I rendered him with the help of God, in the year 1817.

———

Henry Jorger, residing at Reading, brought to me a boy, who suffered extreme pain, caused by wheal in the eye, in the year 1814. In a little more than 24 hours, I, with the help of God, have healed him.

———

John Bayer, son of Jacob Bayer, now living near Read-ing, had an ulcer on the leg, which gave him great pain. I attended him, and in a short time the leg was well. This was in the year 1818.

———

Landlin Gottwald, formerly residing in Reading, had a severe pain in his one arm. In about twenty-four hours I cured his arm.

———

Catharine Meck, at that time in Alsace township, suffered very much from a wheal in the eye. In a little more than twenty-four hours the eye was healed.

———

Mr. Silvis, of Reading, came to my house while engaged at the brewery of my neighbor. He felt great pain in the eye, caused by a wheal. I cured his eye in a little more than 24 hours.

———

Anna Snyder, of Alsace township, had a severe pain in one of her fingers. In a little more than 24 hours she felt relieved.

Michael Hartmann, jr. living in Alsace township, had a child with a very sore mouth. I attended it, and in a little more than 24 hours it was well again.

John Bingemann, at Ruscombmanor, Berks county, had a boy who burnt himself dreadfully. My wife came to that place in the fall of the year 1812. Mortification had already set in—my wife used sympathy for it, and in a short time the mortification was banished. The boy was soon after pelfectly cured, and became well again.—It was about the same time that my wife cured John Bingemann's wife of the wild fire, which she had on a sore leg.

Susanna Gomber, had a severe pain in the head. In a short time I relieved her.

The wife of David Brecht, also felt a severe pain in the head, and was relieved by me in a short time.

John Junkins' daughter and daughter-in-law both suffered very much from pain in the head; and his wife too, had a sore cheek, on which the wild fire had broken out severely. The head-ache of the daughter and the daughter-in-law was banished by me; and the wild fire of the wife was cured in some 7 or 9 hours—the swelled cheek burst open and healed very fast. The woman had been laid up several days already on account of it. The family of Junkins lives at Nackenmixen, but Brecht and Gomber reside in and near Reading. Nackenmixen is in Bucks county. The four last mentioned were cured in the year 1819.

The daughter of John Arnold scalded herself with boiling coffee—the handle of the pot broke off while she was pouring out coffee, and the coffee run over the arm and burnt it severely. I was present and witnessed the accident. I banished the burning—the arm did not get sore at all, and healed in a short time. This was in the year 1815. Mr. Arnold lived near Lebanon, Lebanon county, Penna.

Jacob Stouffer, at Heckak, Bucks county, had a little child who was subject to convulsions every hour. I sold him a book containing the 25 letters; and he was persuaded by his neighbor Henry Frankenfeld, to try these 25 letters.

The result was that the child was instantaneously free from convulsions, and perfectly well. These letters are also to be found in this book.

☞ If any one of the above named witnesses, who have been cured by me and my wife, through the help of God, dares to call me a liar, and deny having been relieved by us, although they have confessed that they had been cured by us—I shall, if it is at all possible, compel them to repeat their confession before a justice of the peace.

A letter to cure rheumatism sold at from one to two dollars, and did not even give directions how to make use of it; these depending on verbal communications. John Allgaier of Reading, had a very sore finger. I used sympathy to banish the wild fire and to cure the finger. The very next morning the wild fire was gone, he scarcely felt any pain, and the finger began to heal very fast. This was in 1819.

☞ This Book is partly derived from a work published by a Gipsey, and partly from secret writings, and collected with much pain and trouble, from all parts of the world, at different periods, by the author, John George Hohman. I did not wish to publish it; my wife, also, was opposed to its publication; but my compassion for my suffering fellow-men was too strong, for I had seen many a one lose his entire sight by a wheal, and his life or limb by mortification. And how dreadfully has many a woman suffered from mother-fits! And I therefore ask thee again, oh friend, male or female, is it not to my everlasting praise, that I have had such books printed? Do I not deserve the rewards of God for it? Where else is the physician that could cure these diseases? Besides that, I am a poor man, in needy circumstances, and it is a help to me if I can make a little money with the sale of my books.

The Lord bless the beginning and the end of this little work, and be with us, that we may not misuse it, and thus commit a heavy sin!—The word *misuse*, means as much as to use it for anything unnecessary. God bless us! Amen. —The word *amen* means as much as that the Lord might bring to pass in reality what had been asked for in prayer.

HOHMAN.

ARTS & REMEDIES.

A good Remedy for Hysterics, (or Mother-Fits,) to be used three times.

Put that joint of the thumb which sits in the palm of the hand on the bare skin covering the small bone which stands out above the pit of the heart, and speak the following at the same time :

Matrix, patrix, lay thyself right and safe,
Or thou or I shall on the third day fill the grave. † † †

Another remedy for Hysterics, and for Colds.

This must be strictly attented to every evening, that is: whenever you pull off your shoes or stockings, run your finger in between all the toes, and smell it. This will certainly effect a cure.

A certain remedy to stop Bleeding—which cures, no matter how far a person be away, if only his first name is rightly pronounced while using it.

Jesus Christ, dearest blood !
That stoppeth the pain, and stoppeth the blood.

In this help you, *(first name)* God the Father, God the Son, God the Holy Ghost. Amen.

A remedy to be used when any one is falling away, and which has cured many persons.

Let the person in perfect soberness and without having conversed with any one, make water in a pot before sunrise; boil an egg in this urine, bore three small holes in this egg with a needle, and carry it to an ant-hill made by big ants ; and the person will feel relieved as soon as the egg is devoured.

Another remedy to be applied when any one is sick ; which has effected many a cure where doctors could not help.

Let the sick person, without having conversed with any one, make water in a bottle before sun-rise, close it up tight, and put it immediately in some box or chest, lock it and stop up the key-hole ; the key must be carried in one of the pockets for three days, as nobody dare have it excepting the person who puts the bottle with urine in the chest or box.

A good remedy for Worms, to be used for men as well as for cattle.

Mary, God's Mother, traversed the land,
Holding three worms close in her hand ;
One was white, the other was black, the third was red.

This must be repeated three times, at the same time stroking the person or animal with the hand ; and at the end of each application strike the back of the person or the animal, to wit : at the first application once, at the second application twice, and at the third application three times ; and then set the worms a certain time, but not less than 3 minutes.

A good remedy against Calumniation or Slander.

If you are calumniated or slandered to your very skin, to your very flesh, to your very bones, cast it back upon the false tongues.   † † †

Take off your shirt, and turn it wrong side out, and then run your two thumbs along your body, close under the ribs, starting at the pit of the heart down to the thighs.

A good remedy for the Fever.

Good morning, dear Thursday! Take away from (name) the 77-fold fevers! Oh! thou dear Lord Jesus Christ, take them away from him!   † † †

This must be used on Thursday for the first time, on Friday for the second time, and on Saturday for the third time; and each time thrice. The prayer of faith has also to be said each time, and not a word dare be spoken to any one until the sun has risen. Neither dare the sick person speak to any one till after sunrise; nor eat pork, nor drink milk, nor cross a running water, for nine days.

A good remedy for the Colic.

I warn ye, ye colic fiends! There is one sitting in judgment, who speaketh: just or unjust. Therefore beware, ye colic fiends!   † † †

To attach a Dog to a person, provided nothing else was used before to effect it.

Try to draw some of your blood, and let the dog eat it along with his food, and he will stay with you. Or scrape the four corners of your table while you are eating, and continue to eat with the same knife after having scraped the corners of the table. Let the dog eat those scrapings, and he will stay with you.

To make a Wand for searching for Iron, Ore, or Water.

On the first night of Christmas, between 11 & 12 o'clock, break off from any tree a young twig of one year's growth, in the three highest names, (Father, Son and Holy Ghost,) at the same time facing towards sunrise. Whenever you apply this wand in searching for anything, apply it three times. The twig must be forked, and each end of the fork must be held in one hand, so that the third and thickest part of it stands up, but do not hold it too tight. Strike the ground with the thickest end, and that which you desire will appear immediately, if there is any in the ground where you strike. The words to be spoken when the wand is thus applied, are as follows:

Archangel Gabriel, I conjure thee in the name of God, the Almighty, to tell me, is there any water here or not? do tell me!   † † †

If you search for iron or ore, you have to say the same, only mention the name of what you are searching for.

A very good remedy for Palpitation of the Heart, and for persons who are Hide-bound.

Palpitation and hide-bound, be off (name) ribs,
Since Christ, our Lord, spoke truth with his lips.

A Precaution against Injuries.

Whoever carries the right eye of a wolf fastened inside of his right sleeve, remains free from all injuries.

How to obtain things which are desired.

If you call upon another to ask for a favor, take care to carry a little of the firefinger-grass with you, and you shall certainly obtain that you desired.

A sure way of catching Fish.

Take rose seed and mustard seed, and the foot of a weasel, and hang these in a net, and the fish will certainly collect there.

A safe remedy for various ulcers, biles, and other defects.

Take the root of iron-weed, and tie it around the neck; it cures running ulcers; it also serves against obstructions in the bladder (stranguary,) and cures the piles, if the roots are boiled in water with honey, and drank; it cleans and heals the lungs and effects a good breath. If this root is planted among grape veins or fruit trees, it promotes the growth very much. Children who carry it, are educated without any difficulty; they become fond of all useful arts and sciences, and grow up joyfully and cheerfully.

A very good remedy for Mortification and Inflammation.

Sanctus Itorius res, call the rest. Here the Mother of God came to his assistance, reaching out her snow-white hand, against the hot and cold brand. † † †

Make three crosses with the thumb. Every thing which is applied in words, must be applied three times, and an interval of several hours must intervene each time, and for the third time it is to be applied the next day, unless where it is otherwise directed.

To prevent wicked or malicious persons from doing you an injury—against whom it is of great power.

Dullix, ix, ux. Yea, you can't come over Pontio; Pontio is above Pilato.   † † †

A very good remedy to destroy Bots or Worms in Horses.

You must mention the name of the horse, and say: "If you have any worms, I will catch you by the forehead. If they be white, brown, or red, they shall and must now all be dead." You must shake the head of the horse three times, and pass your hand over his back three times to and fro.   † † †

To cure the Pollevil in Horses, in two or three applications.

Break off 3 twigs from a cherry tree; one towards morning, one towards evening, and one towards midnight. Cut three small pieces off the hind part of your shirt, and wrap each of those twigs in one of these pieces; then clean the pollevil with the twigs, and lay them under the eaves. The ends of the twigs which had been in the wound must be turned towards the north; after which you must do your business on them, that is to say, you must s—t on them; then cover it, leaving the rags around the twigs. After all this the wound must again be stirred with the three twigs, in one or two days, and the twigs placed as before.

A good remedy for bad Wounds and Burns.

The word of God, the milk of Jesus' Mother, and Christ's blood, is for all wounds and burnings good.   † † †

It is the safest way in all these cases to make the crosses with the hand or thumb three times over the affected parts;

2

that is to say, over all those things to which the three crosses are attached.

A very good remedy for the Wild-fire.

Wild-fire and the dragon, flew over a wagon,
The wild-fire abated, and the dragon skeated.

To stop pains or smarting in a wound.

Cut three small twigs from a tree—each to be cut off in one cut—rub one end of each twig in the wound, and wrap them separately in a piece of white paper, and put them in a warm and dry place.

To destroy Warts.

Roast Chicken-feet and rub the warts with them, then bury them under the eaves.

To banish the Hooping Cough.

Cut three small bunches of hair from the crown of the head of a child that has never seen its father ; sew this hair up in an unbleached rag and hang it around the neck of the child having the hooping cough. The thread with which the rag is sewed must also be unbleached.

Another remedy for the Hooping Cough, which has cured the majority of those who have applied it.

Thrust the child having the hooping-cough three times through a black-berry bush, without speaking or saying anything. The bush, however, must be grown fast at the two ends, and the child must be thrust through three times in the same manner, that is to say, from the same side it was thrust through in the first place.

A good remedy to stop Bleeding.

This is the day on which the injury happened. Blood, thou must stop, until the Virgin Mary bring forth another son.—Repeat these words three times.

15

To banish Convulsive Fevers.

Write the following letters on a piece of white paper, sew it in a piece of linen or muslin, and hang it around the neck until the fever leaves you :

```
A b a x a C a t a b a x
A b a x a C a t a b a x
A b a x a C a t a b a
A b a x a C a t a b
A b a x a C a t a
A b a x a C a t
A b a x a C a
A b a x a C
A b a x a
A b a x
A b a
A b
A
```

A good remedy for the Tooth-ache.

Stir the sore tooth with a needle until it draws blood ; then take a thread and soak it with this blood. Then take vinegar and flower, mix them well so as to form a paste, and spread it on a rag, then wrap this rag around the root of an apple tree, and tie it very close with the above thread, after which the root must be well covered with ground.

How to banish the Fever.

Write the following words upon a paper and wrap it up in knot-grass, (breiten Wegrich,) and then tie it upon the navel of the person who has the fever :

Potmat sineat,
Potmat sineat,
Potmat sineat.

How to walk and step securely in all cases.

Jesus walketh with [name]. He is my head ; I am his limb. Therefore walketh Jesus with [name]. † † †

A very good remedy for the Colic.

Take half a gill of good old rye whiskey, and a pipe full of tobacco; put the whiskey in a bottle, then smoke the tobacco and blow the smoke into the bottle, shake it up well and drink it. This has cured the author of this book, and many others.—Or take a white clay pipe which has turned blackish from smoking, pound it to a fine powder, and take it. This will have the same effect.

A very good Plaster.

I doubt very much whether any physician in the United States can make a plaster equal to this. It heals the white swelling, and has cured the sore leg of a woman who for 18 years had used the prescriptions of doctors in vain.

Take two quarts of cider, one pound of bees-wax, one pound of sheep-tallow, and one pound of tobacco; boil the tobacco in the cider till the strength is out, and then strain it and add the other articles to the liquid, stir it over a gentle fire till all is dissolved.

To make a good Eye Water.

Take four cents worth of white vitriol, four cents worth of prepared spicewort, (calamus root,) four cents worth of cloves, a gill of good whiskey, and a gill of water. Make the calamus fine, and mix all together; then use it after it has stood a few hours.

A very good remedy for the White-Swelling.

Take a quart of unslaked lime, and pour two quarts of water on it; stir it well and let it stand over night. The scum that collects on the lime water must be taken off, and a pint of flax-seed oil poured in, after which it must be stirred until it becomes somewhat consistent; then put it in a pot or pan, and add a little lard and wax, melt it well, and make a plaster, and apply it to the parts affected—the plaster should be renewed every day, or at least every other day until the swelling is gone.

A remedy for Epilepsy, provided the subject had never fallen into fire or water.

Write reversedly or backwards upon a piece of paper: "IT IS ALL OVER!" This is to be written but once upon the paper, then put it in a scarlet-red cloth, and then wrap it in a piece of unbleached linen, and hang it around the neck, on the first Friday of the new moon. The thread with which it is tied must also be unbleached. † † †

Remedy for Burns.

"Burn, I blow on thee!"—It must be blown on three times in the same breath, like the fire by the sun. † † †

To stop Bleeding.

Count backwards from fifty inclusive till you come down to three. As soon as you arrive at three, you will be done bleeding.

A remedy to relieve Pain.

Take a rag which was tied over a wound for the first time, and put it in water together with some copperas; but do not venture to stir the copperas until you are certain of the pain having left you.

A good remedy for the Tooth-ache.

Cut out a piece of greensword (sod) in the morning before sunrise, quite unbeshrewedly, from any place, breathe three times upon it, and put it down upon the same place from which it was taken.

To remove Bruises and Pains.

Bruise, thou shalt not heat;
Bruise, thou shalt not sweat;
Bruise, thou shalt not run,
No more than Virgin Mary shall bring forth
another son. † † †

2*

A remarkable passage from the book of Albertus Magnus.

It says: If you burn a large frog to ashes and mix the ashes with water, you will obtain an ointment that will, if put on any place covered with hair, destroy the hair and prevent it from growing again.

Another passage from the work of Alburtus Magnus.

If you find the stone which a vulture has in his knees, and which you may find by looking sharp, and put it in the vituals of two persons who hate each other, it causes them to make up and be good friends.

To cure Fits or Convulsions.

You must go upon another person's land, and repeat the following words: "I go before another court—I tie up my 77-fold fits." Then cut three small twigs off any tree on the land, in each twig you must make a knot. This must be done on a Friday morning before sunrise, in the decrease of the moon, unbeshrewedly. † † † Then over your body where you feel the fits you make the crosses.—And thus they must be made in all cases where they are applied.

Cure for the Head-ache.

Tame thou flesh and bone, like Christ in Paradise ; and who will assist thee, this I tell thee, (name,) for your repentance-sake. † † † This you must say three times, each time pausing for three minutes, and your head-ache will soon cease. But if your head-ache is caused by strong drink, or otherwise will not leave you soon, then you must repeat those words every minute. This, however, is not often necessary in regard to head-ache.

To mend Broken Glass.

Take common cheese and wash it well, unslaked lime and the white of eggs, rub all these well together until it becomes one mass, and then use it. If it is made right, it will certainly hold.

How to make Cattle return to the same place.

Pull out three small bunches of hair, one between the horns, one from the middle of the back, and one near the tail, and make your cattle eat it in their feed.

Another method of making Cattle return home.

Take a handful of salt, go upon your fields and make your cattle walk three times around the same stump or stone, each time keeping the same direction, that is to say, you must three times arrive at the same end of the stump or stone at which your started from, and then let your cattle lick the salt from the stump or stone.

To prevent the Hessian Fly from Injuring the Wheat.

Take pulverised charcoal, make ley of it, and soak the seed-wheat in it ; take it out of the ley, and on every bushel of wheat sprinkle a quart of urine ; stir it well, then spread it out to dry.

To prevent Cherries from ripening before Martinmas.

Engraft the twigs upon a mulberry tree, and your desire is accomplished.

Stinging Nettle—good for banishing fears and fancies, and to cause fish to collect.

Whenever you hold this weed in your hand together with Millifolia, you are safe from all fears and fancies that frequently deceive men. If you mix it with a decoction of the hemlock, and rub your hands with it, and put the rest in water that contains fish, you will find the fish to collect around your hands. Whenever you pull your hands out of the water, the fish disappear by returning to their former places.

Heliotrope, (sun-flower)—a means to prevent Calumniation.

The virtues of this plant is miraculous, if it be collected in the sign of the lion, in the month of August, and wrapped up in a laurel leaf, together with the tooth of a wolf. Whoever carries this about him, will never be addressed harshly by any one, but all will speak to him kindly and peaceably. And if any thing has been stolen from you, put this under your head during the night, and you will surely see the whole figure of the thief. This has been found true.

To heal a Sore Mouth.

If you have the scurvy, or quinsey too,
I breathe my breath three times into you.

† † †

Swallow-wort,

A means to overcome and end all fighting and anger, and to cause a sick man to weep when his health is restored, or to sing with a cheerful voice when on his death-bed ; also a very good remedy for dim eyes, or shining of the eyes.— This weed grows at the time when the swallows built their nests, or eagles breed. If a man carries this about him, together with the heart of a mole, he shall overcome all fighting and anger. If these things are put upon the head of a sick man, he shall weep at the restoration of his health, and sing with a cheerful voice when he comes to die. When the swallow-wort blooms, the flowers must be pounded up and boiled, and then the water must be poured off into another vessel, and again be placed to the fire and carefully skimmed ; then it must be filtered through a cloth and preserved, and whosoever has dim eyes, or shining eyes, may bathe his eyes with it, and they will become clear and sound.

A good remedy for Consumption.

Consumption, I order thee out of the bones into the flesh, out of the flesh upon the skin, out of the skin into the wilds of the forest.   † † †

For the Hollow Horn in Cows.

Bore a small hole in the hollow horn, milk the same cow, and squirt her milk in the horn ; this is the best cure. Use a syringe to squirt the milk into the horn.

A very good and certain means of destroying the Wheal in the Eye.

Take a dirty plate, if you have none, you can easily dirty one, and the person for whom you are using sympathy shall in a few minutes find the pain much relieved. You must hold that side of the plate or dish, which is used in eating, towards the eye. While you hold the plate before your eye, you must say:

> Dirty plate I press thee,
> Wheal in the eye do flee.

† † †

To make Chickens lay many Eggs.

Take the dung of rabbits, pound it to powder, mix it with bran, wet the mixture till it forms lumps, and feed your chickens with it, and they will keep on laying a great many eggs.

Words to be spoken while making Divinatory Wands.

In making divinatory wands, they must be broken as before directed, and while breaking and before using them, the following words must be spoken:

> Divining wand, do thou keep that power,
> Which God gave unto thee at the very first hour.

How to destroy a Tape Worm.

Worm, I conjure thee by the living God, that thou shalt flee this blood and this flesh, like as God the Lord will flee that judge who judges unjustly, although he might have judged aright. † † †

A good remedy for the Bots in Horses.

Every time you use this, you must stroke the horse down with the hand three times, and lead it about three times, holding its head towards the sun, saying: "The Holy One sayeth: Joseph passed over a field and there he found three small worms; the one being black, another being brown, and the third being red; thus thou shalt die and be dead."

How to cure a Burn.

Three holy men went out walking,
They did bless the heat and the burning;
They blessed that it might not increase;
They blessed that it might quickly cease!
† † †

To cure the Bite of a Snake.

God has created all things, and they were good;
Thou only, serpent, art damned,
Cursed be thou and thy sting.
† † †

Zing, zing, zing!

Security against Mad Dogs.

Dog, hold thy nose to the ground,
God has made me and thee, hound!
† † †

This you must repeat in the direction of the dog; and the three crosses you must make towards the dog, and the words must be spoken before he sees you.

To remove Pain and heal up Wounds with Three Switches.

With this switch and Christ's dear blood,
I banish your pain and do you good!
† † †

Mind it well: you must in one cut, sever from a tree, a young branch pointing towards sunrise, and then make three pieces of it, which you successively put in the wound. Holding them in your hand, you take the one towards your right side first.—Every thing prescribed in this book must be used three times, even if the three crosses should not be affixed. Words are always to have an interval of half an hour, and between the second and third time should pass a whole night, except where it is otherwise directed. The above three sticks, after the end of each has been put into the wound as before directed, must be put in a piece of white paper, and placed where they will be warm and dry.

Remedy for Fever, Worms, and the Colic.

Jerusalem, thou Jewish city,
In which Christ, our Lord, was born,
Thou shalt turn into water and blood,
Because it is for (name,) fever, worms, and colic
good. † † †

How to cure Weakness of the Limbs.

Take the buds of the birch tree, or the inner bark of the root of the tree at the time of the budding of the birch, and make a tea of it, and drink it occasionally through the day. Yet after having used it for two weeks, it must be discontinued for a while, before it is resorted to again; and during the two weeks of its use, it is well at times to use water for a day, instead of the tea.

Another remedy for Weakness.

Take Bittany and St. John's-wort, and put them in good old rye whiskey. To drink some of this in the morning before having taken any thing else, is very wholesome and good. A tea made of the acorns of the white oak is also very good for weakness of the limbs.

A good method of destroying Rats and Mice.

Every time you bring grain into your barn, you must, in putting down the three first sheaves, repeat the following words: "Rats and mice, these three sheaves I give to you, in order that you may not destroy any of my wheat." The name of the kind of grain must always be mentioned.

To make Horses that refuse their Feed to eat again—especially applicable when they are afflicted in this manner on the public roads.

Open the jaws of the horse, which refuses his feed, and knock three times on his palate. This will certainly cause the horse to eat again without hesitation, and to go along willingly.

To cure any Excrescence or Wen on a Horse.

Take any bone which you accidently find, for you dare not be looking for it, and rub the wen of the horse with it ; always bearing in mind that it must be done in the decreasing moon, and the wen will certainly disappear. The bone, however, must be replaced as it was laying before.

How to prepare a good Eye-Water.

Take one ounce of white vitriol and one ounce of sugar of lead, dissolve them in oil of rosemary, and put it in a quart bottle, which you fill up with rose water. Bathe the eyes with it night and morning.

How to cause male or female thieves to stand still, without being able to move backward or forward.

In using any prescriptions of this book in regard to making others stand still, it is best to be walking about; and repeat the following three times :

"Oh Peter, oh Peter, borrow the power from God : what I shall bind with the bands of a christian hand, shall be bound ; all male or female thieves, be they great or small, young or old, shall be spell-bound by the power of God, and not be able to walk forward or backward, until I see them with my eyes, and give them leave with my tongue, except it be that they count for me all the stones that may be between heaven and earth, all rain-drops, all the leaves and all the grass in the world. This I pray for the repentance of my enemies." † † † Repeat your articles of faith and the Lord's prayer.

If the thieves are to remain alive, the sun dare not shine upon them before their release. There are two ways of releasing them, which will be particularly stated : The first is this, that you tell him in the name of St. John to leave: the other is as follows : "The words which have bound thee, shall give thee free." † † †

To cure the Sweeney in Horses.

Take a piece of old bacon, and cut it into small pieces, put them in a pan and roast them well, put in a handful of fish-worms, a gill of oats, and three spoonsful of salt into it; roast the whole of this until it turns black, and then filter it through a cloth; after which you put a gill of soft soap, half a gill of rye whiskey, half a gill of vinegar, and half a gill of the urine of a boy to it; mix it well, and smear it over the part affected with sweeney, on the third, the sixth, and the ninth day of the new moon, and warm it with an oaken board.

How to make Molasses.

Take pumpkins, boil them, press the juice out of them, and boil the juice to a proper consistence. There is nothing else necessary. The author of this book, John George Hohman, has tasted this molasses, thinking it was the genuine kind, until the people of the house told him what it was.

To make good Beer.

Take a handful of hops, five or six gallons of water, about three table-spoonsful of ginger, half a gallon of molasses; filter the water, hops and ginger into a tub containing the molasses.

Cure for the Epilepsy.

Take a turtle-dove, cut its throat, and let the person afflicted with epilepsy drink the blood.

Another way to make Cattle return home.

Feed your cattle out of a pot or kettle used in preparing your dinner, and they will always return to your stable.

A very good remedy to cure Sores.

Boil the bulbs (roots) of the white lilly in cream, and put it on the sore in form of a plaster. Southernwort has the same effect.

A good cure for Wounds.

Take the bones of a calf, and burn them until they turn to power, and then strew it into the wound. This powder

3

prevents the flesh from putrifying, and is therefore of great importance in healing the wound.

To make an Oil out of Paper, which is good for sore eyes.

A man from Germany informed me, that to burn two sheets of white paper would produce about three drops of oil or water, which would heal all sores in or about the eye if rubbed with it. Any affection of the eyes can be cured in this way, as long as the apple of the eye is sound.

To destroy Crab-Lice.

Take capuchin powder, mix it with hog's lard, and smear yourself with it. Or, boil cammock, and wash the place where the lice keep themselves.

To prevent the worst kind of paper from blotting.

Dissolve alum in water, and put it on the paper, and I, Hohman, would like to see who cannot write on it, after it is dried.

A very good remedy for the Gravel.

The author of this book, John George Hohman, applied this remedy, and soon felt relieved. I knew a man who could find no relief from the medicine of any doctor; he then used the following remedy, to wit: he eat every morning seven peach stones before tasting anything else, which relieved him very much; but as he had the gravel very bad, he was obliged to use it constantly. I, Hohman, have used it for several weeks. I still feel a touch of it now and then, yet I had it so badly that I cried out aloud every time I had to make water. I owe a thousand thanks to God and the person who told me of this remedy.

A good remedy for those who cannot keep their water.

Burn a hog's bladder to powder, and take it inwardly.

To destroy Field-Mice and Moles.

Put unslaked lime in their holes, and they will disappear.

To remove a Wen during the crescent moon.

Look over the wen directly towards the moon, and say : " Whatever grows, does grow ; and what diminishes, does diminish." This must be said three times in the same breath.

To remove a Scum or Skin from the Eye.

Before sunrise on St. Bartholomew's day, you must dig up four or five roots of the dandelion weed, taking good care to get the ends of the roots ; then you must procure a rag and a thread that have never been in the water ; the thread, which dare not have a single knot in it, is used in sewing up the roots into the rag, and the whole is then to be hanged before the eye until the scum disappears. The tape by which it it is fastened, must never have been in the water.

For deafness, roaring or buzzing in the ear, & for tooth-ache.

A few drops of refined camphor-oil put upon cotton, and thus applied to the aching tooth, relieves very much. When put in the ear, it strengthens the hearing, and removes the roaring and whizzing in the same.

A good way to cause children to cut their teeth without pain.

Boil the brain of a rabbit, and rub the gums of the children with it, and their teeth will grow without any pain to them.

For Vomiting and Diarrhœa.

Take pulverised cloves and eat them together with bread soaked in red wine, and you will soon find relief. The cloves may be put upon the bread.

To Heal Burns.

Pound or press the juice out of male fern, and put it on the burnt spots, and they will heal very fast. Better yet, however, if you smear the above juice upon a rag, and put that on like a plaster.

*A very good cure for weakness of the limbs, for the purifica-
tion of the blood, for the invigoration of the head & heart,
and to remove giddiness, &c. &c.*

Take two drops of the oil of cloves in a table-spoonful of
white wine, early in the morning, and before eating anything else. This is also good for the mother-pains, and the
colic. The oil of cloves which you buy in the drug stores
will answer the purpose. These remedies are also applicable to cure the cold when it settles in the bowels, and to
stop vomiting. A few drops of this oil poured upon cotton
and applied to the aching teeth, relieves the pain.

For Dysentery and Diarrhœa.

Take the moss off of trees, and boil it in red wine, and
let those that are affected with these diseases, drink it.

Cure for the Tooth-Ache.

Hohman, the author of this book, has cured the severest
tooth-ache more than sixty times, with this remedy; and
out of the sixty times he applied it, it failed but once in affecting a cure. Take blue vitriol and put a small piece of
it in the hollow tooth, yet not too much; spit out the water
that collects in the mouth, and be careful to swallow none.
I do not know whether it is good for teeth that are not hollow, but I should judge it would cure any kind of toothache.

Advise to Pregnant Women.

Pregnant women must be very careful not to use any
camphor; and no camphor should be administered to those
women who have the mother-fits.

Cure for the Bite of a Mad Dog.

A certain Mr. Valentine Kettering, of Dauphin County,
has communicated to the Senate of Pennsylvania, a sure
remedy for the bite of any kind of mad animals. He says
that his ancestors had already used it in Germany 250 years
ago, and that he had always found it to answer the purpose,
during a residence of fifty years in the United States. He

only published it from motives of humanity. This remedy consists in the weed called *Chick-weed.* It is a summer plant, known to the Germans and Swiss by the names of *Gauchneil, Rother Meyer,* or *Rother Huehnerdarm.* In England it is called *Red Pimpernel;* and its botanical name is *Angelica Phonicea.* It must be gathered in June, when in full bloom, and dried in the shade, and then pulverized.— The dose of this for a grown person, is a small table-spoonful, or in weight a drachm and a scruple, at once, in beer or water. For children the dose is the same, yet it must be administered at three different times. In applying it to animals, it must be used green, cut to pieces, and mixed with bran or other feed. For hogs, the pulverised weed is made into little balls by mixing it with flower and water. It can also be put on bread and butter, or in honey, molasses, &c.—The Rev. Henry Muhlenberg says, that in Germany 30 grains of the powder of this weed are given four times a day, the first day, then one dose a day for a whole week; while, at the same time, the wound is washed out with a decoction of the weed, and then the powder strewed in it.— Mr. Kettering says that he in all instances administered but one dose, with the most happy results. This is said to be the same remedy through which the late Doctor William Stoy effected so many cures.

A very good means to increase the growth of Wool on Sheep, and to prevent disease among them.

William Ellis, in his excellent work on the English manner of raising sheep, relates the following : I knew a tenant who had a flock of sheep that produced an unusual quantity of wool. He informed me, that he was in the habit of washing his sheep with butter-milk just after shearing them, which was the cause of the unusual growth of wool; because it is a known fact that buttermilk does not only improve the growth of sheep's wool, but also of the hair of other animals. Those who have no butter-milk may substitute common milk, mixed with salt and water, which will answer nearly as well to wash the sheep just sheared. And I guarantee that by rightly applying this means, you will not

3*

only have a great increase of wool, but the sheep-lice and their entire brood will be destroyed. It also cures all manner of scab and itch, and prevents the sheep from catching cold.

A well-tried Plaster to remove Mortification.

Take six hen eggs and boil them in hot ashes until they are right hard, then take the yellow of the eggs and fry them in a gill of lard until they are quite black, then put a handful of rue with it, and afterwards filter it through a cloth. When this is done, add a gill of sweet oil to it. It will take most effect where the plaster for a female is prepared by a male, and the plaster for a male prepared by a female.

A good remedy for the Poll-Evil in Horses.

Take white turpentine, rub it over the poll-evil with your hand, and then melt it with a hot iron so that it runs into the wound. After this, take neatsfoot oil or goose grease, and rub it into the wound in the same manner, and for three days in succession, commencing on the last Friday of the last quarter of the moon.

For the Scurvy and Sore Throat.

Speak the following, and it will certainly help you : Job went through the land, holding his staff close in the hand, when God the Lord did meet him, and said to him : Job, what art thou grieved at? Job said : Oh God, why should I not be sad? My throat and my mouth are rotting away. Then said the Lord to Job : In yonder valley there is a well, which will cure thee, [name] and thy mouth, and thy throat, in the name of God the Father, the Son, and the Holy Ghost. Amen.

This must be spoken three times in the morning, and three times in the evening ; and where it reads " which will cure," you must blow three times in the child's mouth.

A very good Plaster.

Take wormwood, rue, medels, sheepripwort, pointy plantain, in equal proportions, a larger proportion of beeswax and tallow, and some spirits of turpentine, put it together in a pot, boil it well, and then strain it, and you have a very good plaster.

To stop Bleeding.

I walk through a green forest;
There I find three wells, cool and cold;
   The first is called courage,
   The second is called good,
   And the third is called, stop the blood.

† † †

Another way to stop Bleeding, and to heal Wounds, in man as well as animals.

On Christ's grave there grows three roses; the first is kind, the second is valued among the rulers, and the third says: blood thou must stop, and wound thou must heal.— Every thing prescribed for man in this book, is also applicable to animals.

For gaining a Lawful Suit.

It reads, if any one has to settle any just claim by way of a law suit, let him take some of the largest kind of sage and write the names of the 12 apostles on the leaves, and put them in his shoes before entering the courthouse, and he shall certainly gain the suit.

For the Swelling of Cattle.

To Desh break no Flesh, but to Desh! While saying this run your hand along the back of the animal.   † † †

Note—The hand must be put upon the bare skin in all cases of using sympathetic words.

An easy method of Catching Fish.

In a vessel of white glass must be put: 8 grains of civit, (musk) and as much castorium; 2 ounces of eel-fat, and 4 ounces of unsalted butter; after which the vessel must be well closed, and put in some place where it will keep moderately warm, for nine or ten days, and then the composition must be well stirred with a stick until it is perfectly mixed.

APPLICATION.—1. *In using the hooks*—Worms or insects used for baiting the hooks, must first be moistened with this composition, and then put in a bladder or box, which may be carried in the pocket.

2. *In using the net*—Small balls formed of the soft part of fresh bread must be dipped in this composition, and then by means of thread fastened inside of the net before throwing it into the water.

3. *Catching fish with the hand*—Besmear your legs or boots with this composition before entering the water, at the place where the fish are expected, and they will collect in great numbers around you.

A very good and safe Remedy for Rheumatism.

From one to two dollars have often been paid for this recipe alone, it being the best and surest remedy to cure the rheumatism. Let it be known therefore : Take a piece of cloth, some tape and thread, neither of which must ever have been in water; the thread must not have a single knot in it, and the cloth and tape must have been spun by a child not quite or at least not more than seven years of age. The letter given below must be carefully sowed in the piece of cloth, and tied around the neck, unbeshrewedly, on the first Friday in the decreasing moon ; and immediately after hanging it around the neck, the Lord's prayer and the articles of faith must be repeated. What now follows must be written in the before mentioned letter :

"May God the Father, Son, and Holy Ghost grant it, Amen. Seek immediately, and seek ; thus commandeth the Lord thy God, through the first man whom God did love upon earth. Seek immediately, and seek ; thus commandeth the Lord thy God, through Luke, the Evangelist, and through Paul, the Apostle. Seek immediately, and seek ; thus commandeth the Lord thy God, through the twelve messengers. Seek immediately, and seek ; thus commandeth the Lord thy God, by the first man, that God might be loved. Seek immediately, and convulse ; thus commandeth the Lord thy God, through the Holy Fathers, who have been made by divine and holy writ. Seek immediately, and convulse; thus commandeth the Lord thy God, through the dear and holy angels, and through his paternal and divine Omnipotence, and his heavenly confidence and endurance. Seek immediately, and convulse; thus commandeth the Lord thy God, through the burning oven which was preserved by the blessing of God. Seek immediately, and convulse; thus commandeth the Lord thy God, through all power and might, through the prophet Jonah who was preserved in the belly of the whale for three days and three nights, by the blessing of God. Seek immediately, and convulse; thus commandeth the Lord thy God, through all the power and might which proceed from divine humility, and in all eternity; whereby no harm be done unto † N † nor unto any part of his body, be they the raving convulsions, or the yellow convulsions, or the white convulsions, or the red convulsions, or the black convulsions, or by whatever name convulsions may be called; these all shall do no harm unto thee † N † nor to any part of thy body, nor to thy head, nor to thy neck, nor to thy heart, nor to thy stomach, nor to any of thy reins, nor to thy arms, nor to thy legs, nor to thy eyes, nor to thy tongue, nor to any part or parcel of thy body. This I write for thee † N † in these words, and in the name of God the Father, the Son, and the Holy Ghost, Amen.—God bless it. Amen."

Note.—If any one writes such a letter for another, the Christian name of the person must be mentioned in it; as you will observe, where the N stands singly in the above letter, there must be the name.

A good way to destroy Worms in Bee-Hives.

With very little trouble and at an expense of a quarter dollar, you can certainly free your bee-hives from worms for a whole year. Get from an apothecary store the powder called Pensses Blum, which will not injure the bees in the least. The application of it is as follows: For one bee-hive you take as much of this powder, as the point of your knife will hold, mix it with one ounce of good whiskey, and put it in a common vial, then make a hole in the bee-hive and pour it in thus mixed with the whiskey, which is sufficient for one hive at once. Make the hole so that it can be easily poured in. As said before, a quarter dollar's worth of this powder is enough for one hive.

Recipe for making a paste to prevent gun barrels from rusting, whether iron or steel.

Take one ounce of bear's fat, half an ounce of badger-grease, half an ounce of snake's fat, one ounce of almond oil, and a quarter of an ounce of pulverized indigo, and melt it all together in a new vessel over a fire, stir it well, and put it afterwards into some vessel. In using it, a lump as large as a common nut must be put upon a piece of woolen cloth and then rubbed on the barrel and lock of the gun, and it will keep the barrel from rusting.

To make a Wick which is never consumed.

Take an ounce of asbestos and boil it in a quart of strong ley for two hours; then pour off the ley and clarify what remains by pouring rain water on it three or four times, after which you can form a wick from it which will never be consumed by the fire.

A Morning Prayer, to be spoken before starting on a journey, which will save the person from all mishaps.

I, [here the name is to be pronounced,] will go on a journey to-day; I will walk upon God's way, and walk where God himself did walk, and our dear Lord Jesus Christ, and our dearest Virgin with her dear little babe, with her seven rings and her true things. Oh thou! my dear Lord Jesus Christ, I am thine own, that no dog may bite me, no wolf bite me, and no murderer secretly approach me: Save me, oh my God, from sudden death! I am in God's hands, and there I will bind myself. In God's hands I am by our Lord Jesus' five wounds, that any gun or other arms may not do me any more harm than the virginity of our Holy Virgin Mary was injured by the favour of her beloved Jesus.—After this say three Lord's prayer, the Ava Maria, and the articles of faith.

A safe and approved means to be applied in times of Fire and Pestilence.

Wellcome! thou firey fiend! do not extend further than thou already hast. This I count unto thee as a repentant act, in the name of God the Father, the Son, and the Holy Ghost.

I command unto thee, fire, by the power of God, which createth and worketh every thing, that thou now do cease, and not extend any further; as certainly as Christ was standing on the Jordan's stormy banks being baptised by John, the holy man.

This I count unto thee as a repentant act, in the name of the holy Trinity.

I command unto thee, fire, by the power of God, now to abate thy flames; as certainly as Mary retained her virginity before all ladies who retained theirs, so chaste and pure; therefore, fire, cease thy wrath.

This I count unto thee, fire, as a repentant act, in the name of the most holy trinity.

I command unto thee, fire, to abate thy heat, by the precious blood of Jesus Christ, which he has shed for us, and our sins and transgressions.

This I count unto thee, fire, as a repentant act, in the name of God the Father, the Son, and the Holy Ghost.

Jesus of Nazareth, a king of the Jews, help us from this dangerous fire, and guard this land and its bounds from all epidemic disease and pestilence.

REMARKS.

This has been discovered by a christian Gipsey King of Egypt —Anno 1740, on the 10th of June, six Gipsies were executed on the gallows in the Kingdom of Prussia. The seventh of their party was a man of eighty years of age, and was to be executed by the sword, on the 16th of the same month. But fortunately for him, quite unexpectedly a conflagration broke out, and the old Gipsey was taken to the fire to try his arts; which he successfully done to the great surprise of all present, by bespeaking the conflagration in a manner that it wholely and entirely ceased and disappeared in less than ten minutes. Upon this, the proof having been given in day time, he received pardon and was set at liberty. This was confirmed and attested by the government of the King of Prussia, and the General Superintendent at Kœnigsberg, and given to the public in print. It was first published at Kœnigsberg in Prussia, by Alexander Bausman, anno 1745.

Whoever has this epistle in his house, will be safe from all danger of fire, as well as from lightning. If a pregnant woman carries this letter about her, neither enchantment or evil spirits can injure her or her child. Further, if any body has this letter in his house, or carries it about his person, he will be safe from the injuries of pestilence.

While saying these sentences one must pass three times around the fire. This has availed in all instances.

To prevent Conflagration.

Take a black chicken in the morning or evening, cut its head off and throw it upon the ground; cut its stomach out, yet leave it all together; then try to get a piece of a shirt which was worn by a chaste virgin during her terms, and cut out a piece as large as a common dish from that part which is bloodiest. These two things wrap up together, then try to get an egg which was laid on maunday Thursday. These three things put together in wax; then put them in a pot holding eight quarts, and bury it under the threshhold of your house, with the aid of God, and as long as there remains a single stick of your house together, no conflagration will happen.—If your house should happen to be on fire already in front and behind, the fire will, nevertheless, do no injury to you, nor to your children. This is done by the power of God, and is quite certain and infallible.—If fire should break out unexpectedly, then try to get a whole shirt in which your servant maid had her terms, or a sheet on which a child was born, and throw it into the fire, wrapped up in a bundle, and without saying anything. This will certainly stop it.

To prevent Witches from bewitching Cattle, to be written and placed in the stable; and against Bad Men and Evil Spirits, which nightly torment old and young people, to be written and placed on the bedstead.

" Trotter Head, I forbid thee my house and premises, I forbid thee my horse and cow stable, I forbid thee my bedstead, that thou mayest not breathe upon me : breathe into some other house, until thou hast ascended every hill, until thou hast counted every fence post, and until thou hast crossed every water—And thus dear day may come again into my house, in the name of God the Father, the Son, and the Holy Ghost.   Amen."

This will certainly protect and free all persons and animals from witchcraft.

To prevent bad people from getting about the Cattle.

Take wormwood, gith, five-finger weed, and assafœdita ; three cents worth of each ; the straw of horse-beans, some dirt swept together behind the door of the stable, and a little salt.   Tie these all up together with a tape, and put the bundle in a hole about the threshold over which your cattle pass in and out, and cover it well with lignum vitæ wood. This will certainly be of use.

To Extinguish Fire without Water.

Write the following letters upon each side of a plate, and throw it into the fire, and it will be extinguished forthwith:

```
S A T O R
A R E P O
T E N E T
O P E R A
R O T A S
```

Another Method of stopping Fire.

Our Dear Sarah journeyeth through the land, having a firy, hot brand in her hand.   The firy brand heats ; the firy brand sweats.   Firy brand stop your heat ; firy brand stop your sweat.

How to Fasten or Spell-bind anything.

You say : "Christ's cross and Christ's crown, Christ Jesus' coloured blood, be thou every hour good. God, the Father, is before me ; God, the Son, is beside me ; God, the Holy Ghost, is behind me. Whoever now is stronger than these three persons, may come by day or night, to attack me." † † † Then say the Lord's prayer three times.

Another way of Fastening or Spell-binding.

After repeating the above, you speak : "At every step may Jesus walk with [name]. He is my head, I am his limb ; therefore Jesus be with [name].

A Benediction to prevent Fire.

"The bitter sorrows and the death of our dear Lord Jesus Christ shall prevail. Fire, and wind, and great heat, and all that is within the power of these elements, I command thee through the Lord Jesus Christ, who has spoken to the winds and the waters, and they obeyed him. By these powerful words spoken by Jesus, I command, threaten, and inform thee, fire, flame, and heat, and your powers as elements, to flee forthwith. The holy, rosy blood of our dear Lord Jesus Christ, may rule it. Thou, fire and wind, and great heat, I command thee, as the Lord did by his holy angels command the great heat in the firy oven when those three holy men, Sadrach and his companions, Mesach and Obed Rego, to leave them untouched, as was done accordingly. Thus they shalt abate, thou fire, flame, and great heat, the Almighty God having spoken in creating the four elements, together with heaven and earth : Fiat, Fiat, Fiat ! that is : It shall be, in the name of God, the Father, the Son, and the Holy Ghost. Amen."

How to Relieve Persons or Animals after being Bewitched.

Three false tongues have bound thee, three holy tongues have spoken for thee. The first is God, the father, the second is God, the son, and the third is God, the holy ghost. They will give you blood and flesh, peace and comfort.— Flesh and blood are grown upon thee, born on thee, and lost on thee. If any man trample on thee with his horse, God will bless thee, and the holy Ciprian ; has any woman trampled on thee, God and the body of Mary shall bless thee ; if any servant has given you trouble, I bless thee through God and the laws of heaven ; if any servant maid or woman has led you astray, God and the heavenly constellations shall bless thee. Heaven is above thee, the earth is beneath thee, and thou art between. I bless thee against all tramplings by horses. Our dear Lord Jesus Christ walked about in his bitter afflictions and death ; and all the Jews that had spoken and promised, trembled in their falsehoods and mockery. Look, now trembleth the Son of God, as if he had the itch, said the Jews. And then spake Jesus: I have not the itch, and no one shall have it. Whoever will assist me to carry the cross, him I will free from the itch, in the name of God, the father, the son, and the holy ghost. Amen.

To protect houses and premises against Sickness & Theft.

Ito, alo Massa Dandi Bando, III. Amen.
J. R. N. R. J.

Our Lord Jesus Christ stepped into the hall, and the Jews searched him everywhere. Thus shall those who now speak evil of me with their false tongues, and contend against me, one day bear sorrows, be silenced, dumbstruck, intimidated, and abused, for ever and ever, by the glory of God. The glory of God shall assist me in this. Do thou aid me J. J. J. for ever and ever. Amen.

Against Mishaps and Dangers in the house.

Sanct Matheus, Sanct Marcus, Sanct Lucas, Sanct Johannis.

A Direction for a Gipsy-Sentence, to be carried about the person, as a protection under all circumstances.

Like unto the prophet Jonas, as a type of Christ, who was guarded for three days and three nights in the belly of

a whale, thus shall the Almighty God, as a father, guard
and protect me from all evil.   J. J. J.

Against Evil Spirits and all manner of Witchcraft.

I.

N. I. R.

I.

SANCTUS   SPIRITUS.

I.

N. I. R.

I.

All this be guarded, here in time, and there in eternity.
Amen.

You must write all the above on a piece of white paper,
and carry it about you.—The characters or letters above,
signify : "God bless me here in time, and there eternally."

Against Swellings.

"Three pure Virgins went out on a journey, to inspect a
swelling and sickness.   The first one said : It is hoarse.
The second said : It is not.   The third said : If it is not,
then will our Lord Jesus Christ come."   This must be spok-
en in the name of the Holy Trinity.

Against Adversities and all manner of Contentions.

Power, hero, Prince of Peace, J. J. J.

Against Danger and Death, to be carried about the person.

I know that my Redeemer liveth, and that he will call
me from the grave, &c.

How to Treat a Cow after the Milk is taken from her.

Give to the cow three spoonsful of her last milk, and say
to the spirits in her blood : "Ninny has done it, and I have
swallowed her in the name of God, the father, the son, and
the holy ghost. Amen."—Pray what you choose at the same
time.

Another method of treating a Sick Cow.

J. The cross of Jesus Christ poured out milk ;
J. The cross of Jesus Christ poured out water ;
J. The cross of Jesus Christ has poured them out.

These lines must be written on three pieces of white paper, then take the milk of the sick cow and these three pieces of paper, put them in a pot, and scrape a little of the scull of a criminal on them ; close it well, and put it over a hot fire, and the witch will have to die.—If you take the three pieces of paper, with the writing on them, in your mouth, and go out before your house, speak three times, and then give them to your cattle, you shall not only see all the witches, but your cattle will also get well again.

Against the Fever.

Pray early in the morning, and then turn your shirt around the left sleeve, and say: "turn thou, shirt, and thou, fever, do likewise, turn. [Do not forget to mention the name of the person having the fever.] This I tell thee, for thy repentance sake, in the name of God, the father, the son, and the holy ghost. Amen.—If you repeat this for three successive mornings, the fever will disappear.

To Spell-bind a Thief so that he cannot stir.

This benediction must be spoken a Thursday morning, before sunrise, and in the open air:

"Thus shall rule it God, the father, the son, and the holy ghost, Amen. Thirty-three Angels speak to each other, coming to administer in company with Mary. Then spoke dear Daniel, the holy one: Trust, my dear woman, I see some thieves coming who intend stealing your dear babe ; this I cannot conceal from you. Then spake our dear lady to Saint Peter: I have bound with a band, through Christ's hand ; therefore my thieves are bound even by the hand of Christ, if they wish to steal mine own, in the house, in the chest, upon the meadow or fields, in the woods, in the orchard, in the vineyard, or in the garden, or wherever they intend to steal. Our dear lady said : Whoever chooses may steal ; yet if any one does steal, he shall stand like a buck, be shall stand like a stake, and shall count all the stones upon the earth, and all the stars in the heavens. Thus I give thee leave, and command every spirit to be master over every thief, by the guardianship of Saint Daniel, and by the burden of this world's goods. And the countenance shall be unto thee, that thou canst not move from the spot, as long as my tongue in the flesh shall not give thee leave. This I command thee by the holy virgin Mary, the Mother of God, by the power and might by which he has created heaven and earth, by the host of all the angels, and by all the Saints of God, the father, the son, and the holy ghost, Amen."—If you wish to set the thief free, you must tell him to leave in the name of Saint John.

Another way to Still-bind Thieves.

Ye thieves, I conjure you, to be obedient like Jesus Christ, who obeyed his heavenly father unto the cross, and to stand without moving out of my sight, in the name of the Trinity. I command you by the power of God and the incarnation of Jesus Christ, not to move out of my sight, † † † like Jesus Christ was standing on Jordan's stormy banks to be baptized by John. And furthermore, I conjure you, horse and rider, to stand still and not to move out of my sight, like Jesus Christ did stand when he was about to be nailed to the cross to release the fathers of the church from the bonds of hell. Ye thieves, I bind you with the same bonds with which Jesus our Lord has bound hell; and thus ye shall be bound; † † † and the same words that bind you, shall also release you.

To effect the same in less time.

Thou horseman and footman, you are coming under your hats; you are scattered! With the blood of Jesus Christ, with his five holy wounds, thy barrel, thy gun, and thy pistol are bound; sabre, sword, and knife, are enchanted and bound, in the name of God, the father, the son, and the holy ghost. Amen.

This must be spoken three times.

To Release Spell-bound Persons.

You horseman and footman, whom I here conjured at this time, you may pass on in the name of Jesus Christ, through the word of God and the will of Christ ; ride ye on now and pass.

To Compel a Thief to return Stolen Goods.

Early in the morning before sunrise, you must go to a pear tree, and take with you three nails out of a coffin, or three horse-shoe nails that were never used, and holding these towards the rising sun, you must say :

"Oh thief, I bind thee by the first nail, which I drive into thy scull and thy brain, to return the goods thou hast stolen, to their former place ; thou shalt feel as sick and as anxious to see men, and to see the place you stole from, as felt the desciple Judas after betraying Jerusalem. I bind thee by the other nail, which I drive into your lungs and liver, to return the stolen goods to their former place ; thou shalt feel as sick and as anxious to see men, and to see the place you have stolen from, as did Pilate in the fires of hell. The third nail I shall drive into thy foot, oh thief, in order that thou shalt return the stolen goods to the very same place from which thou hast stolen them. Oh thief, I bind thee, and compel thee, by the three holy nails which were driven through the hands and feet of Jesus Christ, to return the stolen goods to the very same place from which thou hast stolen them." † † † The three nails, however, must be greased with the grease from an excuted criminal or other sinful person.

A Benediction for all purposes.

Jesus, I will arise ; Jesus, do thou accompany me ; Jesus do thou lock my heart into thine, and let my body and my soul be commended unto thee. The Lord is crucified. May God guard my senses that evil spirits may not overcome me, in the name of God, the father, the son, and the holy ghost. Amen.

To Win every Game one engages in.

Tie the heart of a bat with a red silken string to the right arm, and you will win every game at cards you play.

Against Burns.

Our dear Lord Jesus Christ going on a journey, saw a fire-brand burning: it was Saint Lorenzo stretched out on a roast. He rendered him assistance and consolation; he lifted his divine hand, and blessed the brand; he stopped it from spreading deeper and wider. Thus may the burning be blessed in the name of God, the father, the son, and the holy ghost. Amen.

Another Remedy for Burns.

Clear out brand, but never in; be thou cold or hot, thou must cease to burn. May God guard thy blood and thy flesh, thy marrow and thy bones, and every artery great or small—they all shall be guarded and protected in the name of God, against inflammation and mortification, in the name of God the father, the son, and the holy ghost. Amen.

To be given to Cattle, against Witchcraft.

```
S A T O R
A R E P O
T E N E T
O P E R A
R O T A S
```

This must be written on paper and the cattle made to swallow it in their feed.

How to tie up and heal Wounds.

Speak the following: "This wound I tie up in three names, in order that thou mayest take from it, heat, water, falling off of the flesh, swelling, and all that may be injurious about the swelling, in the name of the holy trinity."—This must be spoken three times; then draw a string three times around the wound, and put it under the corner of the house towards the east, and say: "I put thee there, † † † in order that thou mayest take unto thyself the gathered water, the swelling, and the running, and all that may be injurious about the wound. Amen."—Then repeat the Lord's prayer and some good hymn.

4*

To take the Pain out of a Fresh Wound.

Our dear Lord Jesus Christ had a great many biles and wounds, and yet he never had them dressed. They did not grow old, they were not cut, nor were they ever found running. Jonas was blind, and I spoke to the heavenly child, as true as the five holy wounds were inflicted.

A Benediction against Worms.

Peter and Jesus went out upon the fields; they ploughed three furrows, and ploughed up three worms. The one was white, the other was black, and the third one was red. Now all the worms are dead, in the name † † †. Repeat these words three times.

Against every Evil Influence.

Lord Jesus, thy wounds, so red, will guard me against death.

To retain the Right in Court and Council.

Jesus Nazarenus, Rex Judeorum.

First carry these characters with you, written on paper, and then repeat the following words: "I, (name) appear before the house of the judge. Three dead men look out of the window; one having no tongue, the other having no lungs, and the third was sick, blind and dumb."—This is intended to be used when you are standing before a court in your right, and the judge not being favorably disposed towards you. While on your way to the court, you must repeat the benediction already given above.

To stop Bleeding at any time.

As soon as you cut yourself, you must say: "Blessed wound, blessed hour, blessed be the day on which Jesus Christ was born, in the name † † † Amen.

Another way to Stop Blood.

Write the name of the four principle waters of the whole world, flowing out of Paradise, on a paper, namely: Pison,

Gihon, Hedékiel, and Pheat, and put it on the wound. In the first book of Moses, the second chapter, verses 11, 12, 13, you will find them. You will find this effective.

Another similar Prescription.

Breathe three times upon the patient, and say the Lord's prayer three times until the words, "upon the earth," and the bleeding will be stoped.

Another still more certain way to stop Bleeding.

If the bleeding will not stop, or if a vein has been cut, then lay the following on it, and it will stop that hour. Yet if any one does not believe this, let him write the letters upon a knife and stab an irrational animal, and he will not be able to draw blood. And whosoever carries this about him, will be safe against all his enemies:

I. m. I. K. I. B. I. P. a. x. v. ss. Ss. vas I. P. O. unay Lit. Dom. mper vobism.

And whenever a woman is going to give birth to a child, or is otherwise afflicted, let her have this letter about her person; it will certainly be of avail.

A peculiar sign to keep back men and animals.

Whenever you are in danger of being attacked, then carry this sign with you: "In the name of God I make the attack. May it please my Redeemer to assist me. Upon the holy assistance of God I depend entirely; upon the holy assistance of God and my gun I rely very truly. God alone be with us. Blessed be Jesus.

Protection of one's House and Hearth.

Beneath thy guardianship, I am safe against all tempests and all enemies, J. J. J.

These three J's signify *Jesus* three times.

A Charm—to be carried about the person.

Carry these words about you, and nothing can hit you:

Annania, Azaria, and Misael, blessed be the Lord ; for he has redeemed us from hell, and has saved us from death, and he has redeemed us out of the firy furnace, and has preserved us even in the midst of the fire ; in the same manner may it please him, the Lord, that there be no fire :

I.
N. I. R.
I.

To Charm Enemies, Robbers and Murderers.

God be with you, brethern ; stop, ye thieves, robbers, murderers, horsemen, and soldiers, in all humility, for we have tasted the rosy blood of Jesus. Your rifles and guns will be stopped up with the holy blood of Jesus ; and all swords and arms are made harmless by the five holy wounds of Jesus. There are three roses upon the heart of God : the first is beneficent, the other is omnipotent, and the third is his holy will. You, thieves, must therefore stand under it, standing still as long as I will. In the name of God the father, son, and holy ghost, you are conjured and made to stand.

Protection against all kinds of Weapons.

Jesus, God and man, do thou protect me against all manner of guns, fire arms, long or short, of any kind of metal. Keep thou thine fire, like the Virgin Mary, who kept her fire both before and after her birth. May Christ bind up all fire arms after the manner of his having bound up himself in humility, while in the flesh. Jesus, do thou render harmless all arms and weapons, like unto the husband of Mary the mother of God, he having been harmless likewise. Furthermore, do thou guard the three holy drops of blood which Christ sweated on the Mount of Olives. Jesus Christ! do thou protect me against being killed, and against burning fires. Jesus, do thou not suffer me to be killed, much less to be damned, without having received the Lord's supper. May God the father, son, and holy ghost, assist me in this. Amen.

A Charm against Fire-arms.

Jesus passed over the Red Sea, and looked upon the land ; and thus must break all ropes and bands, and thus must break all manner of fire-arms, rifles, guns, or pistols, and all false tougues be silenced. May the benediction of God on creating the first man, always be upon me ; the benediction spoken by God, when he ordered in a dream that Joseph and Mary together with Jesus should flee into Egypt, be upon me always, and may the holy † be ever lovely and beloved in my right hand. I journey through the country at large where no one is robbed, killed, or murdered,— where no one can do me any injury, and where not even a dog could bite me, or any other animal tear me to pieces. In all things let me be protected, as also my flesh and blood, against sins and false tongues which reach from the earth up to heaven, by the power of the four Evangelists, in the name of God the Father, God the Son, and God the Holy Ghost, Amen.

Another for the same.

I, [name,] conjure ye guns, swords, and knives, as well as all other kinds of arms, by the spear that pierced the side of God, and opened it so that blood and water could flow out, that ye do not injure me, a servant of God, in the †††. I conjure ye by Saint Stephan, who was stoned by the virgin, that ye cannot injure me who am a servant of God, in the name of †††. Amen.

A Charm against shooting, cutting or thrusting.

In the name of **J. J. J.** Amen. I, [name,] Jesus Christ is the true salvation ; Jesus Christ governs, reigns, defeats and conquers every enemy, visible or invisible ; Jesus, be thou with me at all times, for ever and ever, upon all roads and ways, upon the water and the land, on the mountain and in the valley, in the house and in the yard, in the whole world wherever I am, stand, run, ride or drive ; whether I sleep or wake, eat or drink, there be thou also, Lord Jesus Christ, at all times, late and early, every hour, every moment ; and in all my goings in or goings out.

Those five holy red wounds, oh Lord Jesus Christ, may they guard me against all fire-arms, be they secret or public, that they cannot injure me, or do me any harm whatever, in the name of †††. May Jesus Christ with his guardianship and protection shield me, (name), always from daily commission of sins, worldly injuries and injustice, from contempt, from pestilence and other diseases, from fear, torture and great suffering, from all evil intentions, from false tongues and old clatter brains; and that no kind of fire-arms can inflict any injury to my body, do thou take care of me † † †. And that no band of thieves, nor Gipsies, highway robbers, incendiaries, witches and other evil spirits may secretly enter my house or premises, nor break in; may the dear Virgin Mary, and all children who are in heaven with God in eternal joys, protect and guard me against them; and the glory of God the Father shall strengthen me, the wisdom of God the Son shall enlighten me, and the grace of God the Holy Ghost shall empower me from this hour unto all eternity. Amen.

To Charm Guns and other Arms.

The blessing which came from heaven at the birth of Christ, be with me (name). The blessing of God at the creation of the first man, be with me; the blessing of Christ on being imprisoned, bound, lashed, crowned so dreadfully and beaten, and dieing on the cross, be with me; the blessing which the Priest spoke over the tender, joyful corpse of our Lord Jesus Christ, be with me; the constancy of the holy Mary and all the Saints of God, of the three holy kings, Casper, Melchior, and Balthasar, be with me; the holy four Evangelists, Matthew, Mark, Luke, and John, be with me; the Archangels St. Michael, St. Gabriel, St. Raphael, and St. Uriel, be with me; the twelve holy messengers of the Patriarchs and all the Hosts of Heaven, be with me; and the inexpressible number of all the Saints, be with me. Amen.

Papa, R. tarn, Tetregammaten Angen. Jesus Nazarenus, Rex Judeorum.

To prevent being Cheated, Charmed, or Bewitched, and to be at all times blessed.

Like unto the cup, and the wine, and the holy supper, which our dear Lord Jesus Christ gave unto his dear disciples on Maunday Thursday, may the Lord Jesus guard me in day time and at night, that no dog may bite me, no wild beast tear me to pieces, no tree fall on me, no water rise against me, no fire-arms injure me, no weapons, no steel, no iron cut me, no fire burn me, no false sentence fall upon me, no false tongue injure me, no rogue enrage me, and that no fiends, no witchcraft and enchantment can harm me.   Amen.

Different Directions to effect the same.

The Holy Trinity guard me, and be and remain with me on the water and upon the land, in the water or in the fields, in cities or villages, in the whole world wherever I am.   The Lord Jesus Christ protect me against all my enemies, secret or public ; and may the Eternal Godhead also guard me, through the bitter sufferings of Jesus Christ ; his holy rosy blood, shed on the cross, assist me. J. J.   Jesus has been crucified, tortured, and died.   These are true words ; and in the same way must all words be efficacious which are here put down, and spoken in prayer by me. This shall assist me that I shall not be imprisoned, bound, or overcome by any one.   Before me all guns and other weapons shall be of no use or power.   Fire-arms, hold your fire in the almighty hand of God.   Thus all fire-arms shall be charmed. †††   When the right hand of the Lord Jesus Christ was fastened to the tree of the cross ; like unto the son of the heavenly father who was obedient unto death, may the eternal Godhead protect me by the rosy blood, by the five holy wounds on the tree of the cross ; and thus must I be blessed and well protected, like the cup and the wine, and the genuine true bread, which Jesus Christ gave to his desciples on the evening of Maunday Thursday. J. J. J.

Another Similar Direction.

The grace of God and his benevolence, be with me (N.)

I shall now ride or walk out ; and I will gird about my loins with a sure ring. So it pleases God, the heavenly father, he will protect me, my flesh and blood, and all my arteries and limbs, during this day and night which I have before me ; and however numerous my enemies might be, they must be dumbstruck, and all become like a dead man, white as snow, so that no one will be able to shoot, cut, or throw at me, nor to overcome me, although he may hold rifle or or steel against whosoever else evil weapons and arms might be called, in his hand. My rifle shall go off like the lightning from heaven, and my sword shall cut like a razor. Then went our dear lady Mary upon a very high mountain ; she looked down into a very dusky valley, and beheld her dear child standing amidst the Jews, harsh, very harsh, because he was bound so harsh, because he was bound so hard ; and therefore may the dear Lord Jesus Christ save me from all that is injurious to me. ††† Amen.

Another Similar Direction.

There walk out during this day and night, that thou may-est not let any of my enemies, or thieves, approach me, if they do not intend to bring me what was spent from the holy alter. Because God, the Lord Jesus Christ, is ascen-ded into heaven in his living body. O Lord, this is good for me this day and night. ††† Amen.

Another one like it.

In the name of God I walk out. God the father be with me, and God the holy ghost be by my side. Whoever is stronger than these three persons, may approach my body and my life ; yet whoso is not stronger than these three, would much better let me be. J. J. J.

A very Safe and reliable Charm.

The peace of our Lord Jesus Christ be with me. [name] Oh shot, stand still! in the name of the mighty prophets Agtion and Elias, and do not kill me! oh shot, stop short! I conjure you by heaven and earth, and by the last judg-ment, that you do no harm unto me, a child of God. †††

Another one like it.

I conjure thee, sword, sabre, or knife, that mightest injure or harm me, by the priest of all prayers, who had gone into the temple at Jerusalem, and said: an edged sword shall pierce your soul that you may not injure me, who am a child of God.

A Very Effective Charm.

I, (name,) conjure thee, sword or knife, as well as all other weapons, by that spear which pierced Jesus' side and opened it to the gushing out of blood and water, that he keep me from injury as one of the servants of God. †††
Amen.

A Good Charm against Thieves.

There are three lilies standing upon the grave of the Lord our God: the first one is the courage of God, the other is the blood of God, and the third one is the will of God. Stand still, thief! No more than Jesus Christ stepped down from the cross, no more shalt thou move from this spot:— this I command thee, by the four evangelists and elements of heaven, there in the river, or in the shot, or in the judgment, or in sight. Thus I conjure you by the last judgment to stand still and not to move, until I see all the stars in heaven, and the sun rises again. Thus I stop thy running and jumping, and command it in the name of †††. Amen.

This must be repeated three times.

How to Recover Stolen Goods.

Take good care to notice through which door the thief passed out, and cut off three small chips from the posts of that door, then take these three chips to a wagon, unbeschrewedly however, take off one of the wheels and put the three chips into the stock of the wheel, in the three highest names, then turn the wheel backwards and say: Thief, thief, thief! Turn back with the stolen goods; thou art forced to do it by the Almighty power of God: ††† God the father calls thee back, God the son turns thee back so that thou must return, and God the holy ghost leads thee back until thou arrive at the place from which thou hast stolen. By the almighty power of God the father thou must come, by the wisdom of God the son thou hast niether peace nor quiet until thou hast returned the stolen goods to their former place, by the grace of God the holy ghost thou must run and jump and canst find no peace or rest until thou arrivest at the place from which thou hast stolen. God the father binds thee, God the son forces thee, and God the holy ghost turns thee back.—(You must not turn the wheel too fast.) Thief, thou must come, ††† thief, thou must come ††† thief, thou must come, †††. If thou art more almighty, thief, thief, thief, if thou art more almighty than God himself, then you may remain where you are. The ten commandments force thee, thou shalt not steal, and therefore thou must come.††† Amen.

A well-tried Charm.

Three holy drops of blood have passed down the holy cheeks of the Lord God, and these three holy drops of blood are placed before the touch-hole. As surely as our dear lady was pure from all men, as surely shall no fire or smoke pass out of this barrel. Barrel, do thou give neither fire, nor flame, nor heat. Now I will walk out, because the Lord God goeth before me, God the son is with me, and God the holy ghost is about me forever.

Another well-tried Charm against Fire-Arms.

Blessed is the hour in which Jesus Christ was born ; blessed is the hour in which Jesus Christ was born ; blessed is the hour in which Jesus Christ has arisen from the dead ; blessed are these three hours over thy gun, that no shot or ball shall fly toward me, and neither my skin, nor my hair, nor my blood, nor my flesh, be injured by them, and that no kind of weapon or metal shall do me any harm, so surely as the Mother of God shall not bring forth another son. †††. Amen.

A Charm to gain advantage of a man of superior strength.

I, [name,] breathe upon thee. Three drops of blood I take from thee ; the first out of thy heart, the other out of thy liver, and the third out of thy vital powers ; and in this I deprive thee of thy strength and manliness.

Hbbi Massa danti Lantien. I. I. I.

A Recipe for destroying Spring-Tails or Ground Fleas.

Take the chaff upon which children have been laying in their cradles, or take the dung of horses, and put that upon the field, and the spring-tails or ground-fleas will no longer do you any injury.

A Benediction for and against all Enemies.

The cross of Christ be with me ; the cross of Christ overcomes all water and every fire ; the cross of Christ overcomes all weapons ; the cross of Christ is a perfect sign and blessing to my soul. May Christ be with me and my body during all my life, at day and at night. Now I pray, I, [name,] pray God the father for the soul's sake, and I pray God the son for the father's sake, and I pray God the holy ghost for the Father's and the Son's sake, that the holy corpse of God may bless me against all evil things, words, and works. The cross of Christ open unto me future bliss ; the cross of Christ banish all evil from me ; the cross of Christ be with me, above me, before me, behind me, beneath me, aside of me, and everywhere, and before all my enemies, visible and invisible ; these all flee from me as soon as they but know or hear. Enoch and Elias, the two prophets, were never imprisoned, nor bound, nor beaten, and came never out of their power : thus no one of my enemies must be able to injure or attack me in my body or my life, in the name of God the Father, the Son, and the Holy Ghost. Amen.

A Benediction against Enemies, Sickness and Misfortunes.

The blessing which came from heaven, from God the father, when the true living Son was born, be with me at all times; the blessing which God spoke over the whole human race, be with me always. The holy cross of God, as long and as broad, as the one upon which God suffered his blessed, bitter tortures, bless me to-day and forever. The three holy nails which were driven through the holy hands and feet of Jesus Christ, shall bless me to-day and forever. The bitter crown of thorns which was forced upon the holy head of Christ, shall bless me to-day and forever. The spear by which the holy side of Jesus was opened, shall bless me to-day and forever. The rosy blood protect me from all my enemies, and from every thing which might be injurious to my body or soul, or my worldly goods. Bless me, oh ye five holy wounds, in order that all my enemies may be driven away and bound, while God has encompassed all Christendom. In this shall assist me God the Father, the Son, and the Holy Ghost. Amen.—Thus must I, (N.) be blessed as well and as valid as the cup and the wine, and the true, living bread which Jesus gave his desciples on the evening of Maunday Thursday. All those that hate you, must be silent before me; their hearts are dead in regard to me; and their tongues are mute, so that they are not at all able to inflict the least injury upon me, or my house, or my premises: And likewise, all those who intend attacking and wounding me with their arms and weapons, shall be defenceless, weak, and conquered before me. In this shall assist me the holy power of God, which can make all arms or weapons of no avail. All this in the name of God the father, the son, and the holy ghost. Amen.

THE TALISMAN.

It is said that any one going out hunting and carrying it in his game bag, cannot but shoot something worth while, and bring it home.

An old hermit once found an old, lame huntsman in a forest, laying beside the road, and weeping. The hermit asked him the cause of his dejection. Ah me, thou man of God, I am a poor unfortunate being; I must annually furnish my lord with as many deer, and hares, and partridges, as a young and healthy huntsman could hunt up, or else I will be discharged from my office; now I am old and lame, besides game is getting scarce, and I cannot follow it up any longer as I ought to; and I know not what will become of me.—Here the old man's feelings overcome him, and he could not utter another word. The hermit, upon this, took out a small piece of paper, upon which he wrote some words with a pencil, and handing it to the huntsman, he said: there, old friend, put this in your game-bag whenever you go out hunting, and you shall certainly shoot something worth while, and bring it home too; yet be careful to shoot no more than you necessarily need, nor to communicate it to any one that might misuse it, on account of the high meaning contained in these words. The hermit then went on his journey, and after a little the huntsman also arose, and without thinking of any thing particular, he went into the woods, and had scarcely advanced a hundred yards, when he shot as fine a roe-buck as he ever saw in his life.

This huntsman was afterwards and during his whole life-time lucky in his hunting, so much so that he was considered one of the best hunters in that whole country. The following is what the hermit wrote on the paper:

Ut nemo in sense tentat, descendere nemo.

* * *
† ☩ †

At precedenti spectatur mantica tergo.

The best argument is to try it.

To prevent any one from Killing Game.

Pronounce the name, as for instance *Jacob Wohlgemuth*, shoot whatever you please; shoot but hair and feathers with and what you give to poor people. ††† Amen.

To Compel a Thief to Return Stolen Goods.

Walk out early in the morning, before sunrise, to a Juniper tree, and bend it with the left hand towards the rising sun, while you are saying: Juniper tree, I shall bend and

5*

squeeze thee, until the thief has returned the stolen goods to the place from which he took them.—Then you must take a stone and put it on the bush, and under the bush and the stone you must place the scull of a malefactor. † † † Yet you must be careful in case the thief return the stolen goods, to unloose the bush and replace the stone where it was before.

A Charm against Powder and Ball.

The heavenly and holy trumpet blow every ball and misfortune away from me. I seek refuge beneath the tree of life which bears twelvefold fruits. I stand behind the holy altar of the christian church. I commend myself to the holy trinity. I, [name,] hide myself beneath the holy corpse of Jesus Christ. I commend myself unto the wounds of Jesus Christ, that the hand of no man might be able to sieze me, or to bind me, or to cut me, or to throw me, or to beat me or to overcome me in any way whatever, so help me, [N.]

☞ Whoever carries this book with him, is safe from all his enemies, visible or invisible; and whoever has this book with him, cannot die without the holy corpse of Jesus Christ, nor drownd in any water, nor burn up in any fire, nor can an unjust sentence be passed upon him. So help me. † † †

UNLUCKY DAYS,
To be found in each Month.

January 1 2 3 4 6 11 12.   July 17 21.
February 1 17 18.   August 20 21.
March 14 16.   September 10 18.
April 10 17 18.   October 6.
May 7 8.   November 6 10.
June 17.   December 6 11 15.

Whoever is born upon one of these days, is unfortunate and suffers from poverty; and whoever takes sick on one of these days, seldom recovers health; and those who engage or marry on these days, become very poor and miserable. Neither is it advisable to move from one house to another, nor to travel, nor to bargain, nor to engage in a law-suit, on one of these days.

The Signs of the Zodiac must be observed by the course of the moon, as they are daily given in common almanacs.

If a cow calves in the sign of the Virgin, the calf will not live one year; if it happens in the Scorpion, it will die much sooner; therefore no one should be weened off in these signs, nor in the sign of the Capricorn or Aquarius, and they will be in less danger from mortal inflammation.

This is the only piece extracted from a centennial almanac imported from Germany, and there are many who believe in it.

HOHMAN.

In conclusion the following Morning Prayer is given, which is to be spoken before entering upon a Journey. It protects against all manner of bad luck.

Oh Jesus of Nazereth, King of the Jews, yea, a King over the whole world, protect me, (name,) during this day and night, protect me at all times by thy five holy wounds, that I may not be siezed and bound. The holy trinity guard me, that no gun, fire-arm, ball, or lead, shall touch my body; and that they shall be weak like the tears and the bloody sweat of Jesus Christ, in the name of God the father, the son, and the holy ghost. Amen.

APPENDIX.

The following Remedy for Epilepsy was published in the Lancaster, (Pa.) papers, in the year 1828.

TO SUFFERING HUMANITY.

We ourselves know of many unfortunate beings who are afflicted with Epilepsy—yet how many more may be in the country who have perhaps already spent their fortunes in seeking aid in this disease, without gaining relief. We have now been informed of a remedy which is said to be infallible, and which has been adopted by the most distinguished physicians in Europe, and has so well stood the test of repeated trials, that it is now generally applied in Europe. It directs a bedroom for the sick person to be fitted up over the cow stable, where the patient must sleep at night, and should spend the greater part of his time during the day in it. This is easily done by building a regular room over the stable. Then care is to be taken to leave an opening in the ceiling of the stable, in such a manner that the evaporation from the same can pass into the room, while, at the same time, the cow may inhale the perspiration of the sick person. In this way the animal will gradually attract the whole disease, and be affected with arthritic attacks, and when the patient has entirely lost them, the cow will fall dead to the ground. The stable must not be cleaned during the operation, though fresh straw or hay may be put in ; and, of course, the milk of the cow, as long as she gives any, must be thrown away as useless.

[*Lancaster Eagle.*

A Salve to Heal up Wounds.

Take tobacco, green or dry; if green, a good handful; if dry, 2 ounces; together with this take a good handful of elder leaves, fry them well in butter, press it through a cloth, and you may use it as a salve. This will heal up a wound in a short time.

Or go to a white oak tree that stands pretty much isolated, and scrape off the rough bark from the eastern side of the tree, then cut off the thinner bark, break it into small pieces, and boil it until all the strength is drawn out, strain it through a piece of linnen, and boil it again, until it becomes as thick as tar; then take out as much as you need, and put to it an equal proportion of sheep tallow, rosin and wax, and work them together until they form a salve. This salve you put on a piece of linnen, very thinly spread, and lay it on the wound, renewing it occasionally till the wound is healed up.

Or take a handful of parseley, pound it fine, and work it to a salve with an equal proportion of fresh butter. This salve prevents mortification and heals very fast.

PEACHES.

The flowers of the peach tree, prepared like salad, opens the bowels, and is of use in the dropsy. Six or seven pealed kernels of the peach stone, eaten daily, will ease the gravel; they are also said to prevent drunkenness, when eaten before meals.

Whoever loses his hair, should pound up peach kernels, mix them with vinegar, and put them on the bald place.

The water distilled from peach flowers, opens the bowels of infants, and destroys their worms.

SWEET OIL.

Sweet oil possesses a great many valuable properties, and it is therefore adviseable for every head of a family to have it at all times about the house, in order that it may be applied in cases of necessity. Here follow some of its chief virtues:

It is a sure remedy, internally as well as externally, in all cases of inflammation, in men and animals.

Internally, it is given to allay the burning in the stomach, caused by strong drink or by purging too severely, or by poisonous medicines. Even if pure poison has been swallowed, vomiting may be easily produced by one or two wine glasses of sweet oil, and thus the poison will be carried off, provided it has not already been too long in the bowels; and after the vomiting, a spoonful of the oil should be taken every hour until the burning caused by the poison, is entirely allayed.

Whoever is bit by a snake, or by any other poisonous animal, or by a mad dog, and immediately takes warmed sweet oil, and washes the wound with it, and then puts a rag, three or four times doubled up, and well soaked with oil, on the wound every three or four hours, and drinks a couple of spoonsful of the oil, every four hours, for some days, will surely find out what peculiar virtues the sweet oil possesses in regard to poisons.

In Dysentery, sweet oil is likewise a very useful remedy, when the stomach has first been cleansed by Rheubarb or some other suitable purgative, and then a few spoonsful of sweet oil should be taken every three hours. For this purpose, however, the sweet oil should have been well boiled and a very little hartshorn be mixed with it. This boiled sweet oil is also serviceable in all sorts of bowel complaints and in colics; or when any one receives internal injury as from a fall, a few spoonsful of it should be taken every two hours: for it allays the pain, scatters the coadjulated blood, prevents all inflammation, and heals gently.

Externally, it is applicable in all manner of swellings; it softens, allays the pain, and prevents inflammation.

Sweet oil and white lead ground together, makes a very good salve, which is applicable in burns or scalds. This salve is also excellent against infection from poisonous weeds or waters, if it is put on the infected part as soon as it is noticed.

If sweet oil is put in a large glass, so as to fill it about one half full, and the glass is then filled up with the flowers of the St. Johnswort, and well covered and placed in the

6

sun for about four weeks, the oil proves then, when distilled, such a valuable remedy for all fresh wounds in men and animals, that no one can imagine its medicinal powers who has not tried it. This should at all times be found in a well conducted household. In a similar manner, an oil may be made of white lilies, which is likewise very useful to soften hardened swellings and burns, and to cure the sore breasts of women.

CURE FOR DROPSY.

Dropsy is a disease derived from a cold humidity, which passes through the different limbs to such a degree that it either swells the whole or a portion of them. The usual symptoms and precursers of every case of dropsy, are the swelling of the feet and thighs, and then of the face; besides this the change of the natural colour of the flesh into a dull white, with great thirst, loss of appetite, costiveness, sweating, throwing up of slimy substances, but little urine, laziness and aversion to exercise.

Physicians know three different kinds of dropsy, which they name :

1. *Anasarca*, when the water penetrates between the skin and the flesh over the whole body, and all the limbs, and even about the face, and swells them.

2. *Ascites*, when the belly and thighs swell, while the upper extremities dry up.

3. *Tympanites*, caused rather by wind than water. The belly swells up very hard, the navel is forced out very far, and the other members fall away. The belly becomes so much inflated, that knocking against it causes a sound like that of a large drum, and from this circumstance its name is derived.

The chief thing in curing dropsy, rests upon three points, namely:

1. To reduce the hardness of the swelling which may be in the bowels or other parts.

2. To endeavor to scatter the humours.

3. To endeavor to pass them off either through the stool or through the urine.

The best cure therefore must chiefly consist in this : To avoid as much as possible all drinking, and use only dry vituals ; to take moderate exercise, and to sweat and purge the body considerably.

If any one feels symptoms of dropsy, or while it is yet in its first stages, let him make free use of the sugar of the herb called *Fumatory*, as this purifies the blood ; and the *Euphrasy* sugar to open the bowels.

A CURE FOR DROPSY.—*(Said to be Infallible.)*

Take a jug of stone or earthen ware, and put four quarts of strong healthy cider into it ; take two handsful of parsely roots and tops, cut it fine ; a handful of scraped horseraddish, two table-spoonsful of bruised mustard seed, half an ounce of squills, and half an ounce of juniper berries ; put all these in the jug, and place it near the fire for 24 hours, so as to keep the cider warm, and shake it up often ; then strain it through a cloth and keep it for use.

To a grown person give half a wine glass full three times a day, on an empty stomach. But if necessary you may increase the dose, although it must decrease again as soon as the water is carried off ; and, as stated before, use dry vituals and exercise gently.

This remedy has cured a great many persons, and among others a woman of 70 years of age, who had the dropsy so badly, that she was afraid to get out of bed, for fear her skin might burst, and whom it was thought could not live but a few days. She used this remedy according to the directions given, and in less than a week the water had passed off her, the swelling of her stomach fell, and in a few weeks afterwards she again enjoyed perfect health.

Or : Drink for a few days very strong Bohea tea, and eat the leaves of it. This simple means is said to have carried away the water from some persons in three or four days, and freed them from the swelling, although the disease had reached the highest pitch.

Or : Take three spoonsful of rape seed, and half an ounce of clean gum myrrh, put these together in a quart of good old wine, and let it stand over night in the room, keeping it well covered. Aged persons are to take 2 spoonsful of this an hour after supper, and the same before going to bed ; younger persons must diminish the quantity according to their age, and continue the use of it as long as necessary.

Or: Take young branches of spruce pine, cut them into small pieces, pour water on them and let them boil a while, then pour it into a large tub, take off your clothes, and sit down over it, covering yourself and the tub with a sheet or blanket, to prevent the vapour from escaping. When the water begins to cool, let some one put in hot bricks ; and when you have thus been sweating for a while, wrap the sheet or blanket close around you and go to bed with it. A repetition of this for several days will free the system from all water.

The following Valuable Recipes, not in the original work of Hohman, are added by the publishers.

CURE FOR DROPSY.

Take of the broom-corn seed, well powdered and sifted, one drachm. Let it steep twelve hours in a wine glass and a half of good rich wine, and take it in the morning fasting, having first shaken it so that the whole may be swallowed. Let the patient walk after it, if able, or let him use what exercise he can without fatigue, for an hour and a half; after which let him take 2 oz. of olive oil; and not eat or drink any thing in less that half an hour afterwards. Let this be repeated every day, or once in three days, and not oftener, till a cure is effected; and do not let blood, or use any other remedy during the course.

Nothing can be more gentle and safe than the operation of this remedy. If the dropsy is in the body, it discharges it by urine, without any inconvenience: if it is between the skin and flesh, it causes blisters to rise on the legs, by which it will run off; but this does not happen to more than one in thirty: and in this case no plasters must be used, but apply red cabbage leaves. It cures dropsy in pregnant women, without injury to the mother or child. It also alleviates asthma, consumption, and disorders of the liver.

REMEDY FOR THE LOCK JAW.

We are informed by a friend that a sure preventive against this terrible disease, is, to take some soft soap, and mix it with a sufficient quantity of pulverized chalk, so as to make it of the consistency of buckwheat batter; keep the chalk moistened with a fresh supply of soap until the wound begins to discharge, and the patient finds relief. Our friend stated to us that explicit confidence may be placed in what he says, that he has known several cases where this remedy has been successfully applied. So simple and so valuable a remedy, within the reach of every person, ought to be generally known.

[N. Y. Evening Post.

FOR THE STING OF A WASP OR BEE.

A Liverpool paper states as follows:—" A few days ago happening to be in the country, we witnessed the efficacy of the remedy for the sting of a wasp mentioned in one of our late papers. A little boy was stung severely and was in great torture, until an onion was applied to the part affected, when the cure was instantaneous. This important and simple remedy cannot be too generally known, and we pledge ourselves to the fact above stated."

INDEX:

6*

APPENDIX.

You have beheld the book as it first appeared—
shaped by its time,
marked by its history,
and carried forward by those who found comfort in its words.

Now you step from the world of 1820
into the clarity of the present.
As the facsimile preserves the past,
so the typeset edition offers understanding.
May this transition be a blessing to your mind and heart.
May the same Spirit who guided those before us
grant you insight as you continue.
May the words ahead be clear,
the meaning be plain,
and the blessings be fresh and alive.

As you pass from the old to the renewed,
may God's peace accompany you.
May His light rest upon your reading,
and may the friendship of this book—
old in its origin, new in its rendering—
stand beside you in strength and gentleness.

Proceed now with an open mind and a steady spirit,
and may the blessings of the Lord
be with you in the pages that follow.

On the Word "Powwow" and Its Misapplication

Beginning in the early twentieth century, some publishers reissued *The Long Lost Friend* under the title "**Pow-Wows; or, The Long Lost Friend.**" The change was not based on history, scholarship, or cultural accuracy. It was a marketing decision, reflecting the careless language of that era rather than the truth of the tradition.

The term "**powwow**" originally comes from Eastern Algonquian languages and referred to **a healer, shaman, or spiritual advisor within Native American communities.** These ceremonies, practices, and roles are sacred and culturally specific; they have nothing to do with German immigrant folk-Christianity, Braucherei, or the rural Pennsylvania Dutch tradition.

Hohman's work is **Christian, German, scriptural**, and **European in origin**, drawn from a lineage of blessings, psalms, and devotional folk remedies passed down through families and church communities.

The use of "powwow" to describe this tradition was:

- **not accurate**,
- **not respectful**, and
- **not reflective of Native American spirituality or practice.**

This edition restores the proper lineage:
rooted in **Christian folk practice**, shaped by **Pennsylvania German culture**, and grounded in **scripture**, **prayer**, and **daily devotional life**, not in Native American ceremonial tradition.

Where earlier publishers blurred lines, this edition draws them clearly.

THE

LONG LOST FRIEND.

OR

Faithful & Christian Instructions

CONTAINING

WONDEROUS AND WELL-TRIED

ARTS & REMEDIES,

FOR

MAN AS WELL AS ANIMALS.

WITH MANY PROOFS

Of their virtue and efficacy in healing diseases, &c. the greater part of which was never published until they appeared in print for the first time in the U. S. in the year 1820.

LITERALLY TRANSLATED FROM THE GERMAN WORK OF

JOHN GEORGE HOHMAN,

Near Reading, Alsace Township, Berks County, Penn.

HARRISBURG, PA.—1850.

PREFACE.

—◆—

THE author should have preferred writing no preface whatever to this little book, were it not indispensably necessary, in order to meet the erroneous views some men entertain in regard to works of this character. The majority, undoubtedly, approve of the publication and sale of such books, yet some are always found who will persist in denouncing them as something wrong. This latter class I cannot help but pity for being so far led astray; and I earnestly pray every one who might find it in his power, to bring them from off their ways of error. It is true, whosoever taketh the name of Jesus in vain, committeth a great sin. Yet is it not expressly written in the 50th Psalm, according to Luther's translation: "Call upon me in the day of trouble: I will deliver thee, and thou shalt glorify In the Catholic translation, the same passage is found in the 49th Psalm, reading thus: "Call upon me in the day of thy trouble, and I will deliver thee, and thou shalt glorify me."

Where is the doctor who has ever banished the panting or palpitation of the heart and hideboundeness? Where is the doctor who ever banished a wheal? Where is the doctor who ever banished the mother-fits? Where is the doctor who can cure mortification when it once seizes a member of the body? All these cures, and a great many more misterious things are contained in this book; and its author could take an oath at any time upon the fact of his having successfully applied many of the prescriptions on its pages. I say: Any and every man who knowingly neglects using this book in saving the eye, or the leg, or any other limb of his fellow-man, is guilty of the loss of such limb, and thus committing a sin, he may forfeit to himself all hope of heaven. Such men refuse to call upon the Lord in their trouble, although he especially commands it. If men were not allowed to use sympathetic words, nor the name of the Most High, it would certainly not have been revealed to them; and what is more, the Lord would not help where they are made use of. God can in no manner be forced to intercede where it is not his divine pleasure. Another thing I have to notice here: there are men who will say, if one has used sympathetic words in vain, the medicines of doctors could not avail any, because the words did not effect a cure. This is only the excuse of physicians; because whatever cannot be cured by sympathetic words can much less be cured by any doctor's craft or cunning. I could name at any time that catholic priest whose horse was cured with mere words; and I could also give the name of the man who done it. I knew the priest well; he formerly resided in Westmoreland county. If it was desired, I could also name a reformed preacher, who cured several persons of the fever, merely by writing them some tickets for that purpose; and even the names of those persons I could mention. This preacher formerly resided in Berks county.—If men but use out of this book what they actually need, they surely commit no sin; yet wo unto those who are guilty that any one loses his life in consequence of mortification, or loses a limb, or the sight of the eye! Wo unto those who misconstrue these things at the moment of danger, or who follow the ill advise of any preacher who might teach them not to mind what the Lord says in the 50th Psalm: "Call upon me in the day of trouble: I will deliver thee, and thou shalt glorify me."—Wo unto those who in obeying the directions of a preacher, neglect using any means offered by this book against mortification, or inflammation, or the wheal. I am willing to follow the preacher in all reasonable things, yet when I am in danger and he advises me not to use any prescriptions found in this book, in such a case I shall not obey him. And wo also unto those who use the name of the Lord in vain and for trifling purposes.

I have given many proofs of the usefulness of this book, and I could yet do it at any time. I sell my books publicly, and not secretly, as other mystical works are sold. I am willing that my books should be seen by every body, and I shall not secrete or hide myself from any preacher. I, Hohman, too, have some knowledge of the scriptures, and I know when to call and pray unto the Lord for assistance. The publication of books (provided they are useful and morally right,) is not prohibited in the United States, as is the case in other countries where kings and despots hold tyrannical sway over the people. I place myself upon the broad platform of the liberty of the press and of conscience, in regard to this useful book, and it shall ever be my most heartfelt desire that all men might have an opportunity of using it to their good, in the name of Jesus.

Given at Rosenthal, near Reading, Berks county, Penn. on the 31st day of July, in the year of our Lord 1819.

JOHN GEORGE HOHMAN,
Author and original publisher of this book.

NOTE.

There are many in America who believe neither in a hell nor in heaven; but in Germany there are not so many of these persons found. I, Hohman, ask: Who can immediately banish the wheal, or mortification? I reply, and I, Hohman, say: All this is done by the Lord.—Therefore a hell and a heaven must exist; and I think very little of any one who dares to deny it.

TESTIMONIALS,

Which go to show at any time, that I, Hohman, have successfully applied the prescriptions of this book.

Benjamin Stoudt, the son of a Lutheran school-master, at Reading, suffered dreadfully from a wheal in the eye.—In a little more than 24 hours, this eye was as sound as the other one, by the aid I rendered him with the help of God, in the year 1817.

Henry Jorger, residing at Reading, brought to me a boy, who suffered extreme pain, caused by wheal in the eye, in the year 1814. In a little more than 24 hours, I, with the help of God, have healed him.

John Bayer, son of Jacob Bayer, now living near Reading, had an ulcer on the leg, which gave him great pain. I attended him, and in a short time the leg was well. This was in the year 1818.

Landlin Gottwald, formerly residing in Reading, had a severe pain in his one arm. In about twenty-four hours I cured his arm.

Catharine Meck, at that time in Alsace township, suffered very much from a wheal in the eye. In a little more than twenty-four hours the eye was healed.

Mr. Silvis, of Reading, came to my house while engaged at the brewery of my neighbor. He felt great pain in the eye, caused by a wheal. I cured his eye in a little more than 24 hours.

Anna Snyder, of Alsace township, had a severe pain in one of her fingers. In a little more than 24 hours she felt relieved.

Michael Hartmann, jr. living in Alsace township, had a child with a very sore mouth. I attended it, and in a little more than 24 hours it was well again.

John Bingemann, at Ruscombmanor, Berks county, had a boy who burnt himself dreadfully. My wife came to that place in the fall of the year 1812. Mortification had already set in—my wife used sympathy for it, and in a short time the mortification was banished. The boy was soon after pelfectly cured, and became well again.—It was about the same time that my wife cured John Bingemann's wife of the wild fire, which she had on a sore leg.

Susanna Gomber, had a severe pain in the head. In a short time I relieved her.

The wife of David Brecht, also felt a severe pain in the head, and was relieved by me in a short time.

John Junkins' daughter and daughter-in-law both suffered very much from pain in the head; and his wife too, had a sore cheek, on which the wild fire had broken out severely. The head-ache of the daughter and the daughter-in-law was banished by me; and the wild fire of the wife was cured in some 7 or 9 hours—the swelled cheek burst open and healed very fast. The woman had been laid up several days already on account of it. The family of Junkins lives at Nackenmixen, but Brecht and Gomber reside in and near Reading. Nackeninixen is in Bucks county. The four last mentioned were cured in the year 1819.

The daughter of John Arnold scalded herself with boiling coffee—the handle of the pot broke off while she was pouring out coffee, and the coffee run over the arm and burnt it severely. I was present and witnessed the accident. I banished the burning—the arm did not get sore at all, and healed in a short time. This was in the year 1815. Mr. Arnold lived near Lebanon, Lebanon county, Penna.

Jacob Stouffer, at Heckak, Bucks county, had a little child who was subject to convulsions every hour. I sold him a book containing the 25 letters; and he was persuaded by his neighbor Henry Frankenfeld, to try these 25 letters. The result was that the child was instantaneously free from convulsions, and perfectly well. These letters are also to be found in this book.

☞ If any one of the above named witnesses, who have been cured by me and my wife, through the help of God, dares to call me a liar, and deny having been relieved by us, although they have confessed that they had been cured by us—I shall, if it is at all possible, compel them to repeat their confession before a justice of the peace.

A letter to cure rheumatism sold at from one to two dollars, and did not even give directions how to make use of it; these depending on verbal communications. John Allgaier of Reading, had a very sore finger. I used sympathy to banish the wild fire and to cure the finger. The very next morning the wild fire was gone, he scarcely felt any pain, and the finger began to heal very fast. This was in 1819.

☞ This Book is partly derived from a work published by a Gipsey, and partly from secret writings, and collected with much pain and trouble, from all parts of the world, at different periods, by the author, John George Hohman. I did not wish to publish it; my wife, also, was opposed to its publication; but my compassion for my suffering fellowmen was too strong, for I had seen many a one lose his entire sight by a wheal, and his life or limb by mortification. And how dreadfully has many a woman suffered from mother-fits! And I therefore ask thee again, oh friend, male or female, is it not to my everlasting praise, that I have had such books printed? Do I not deserve the rewards of God for it? Where else is the physician that could cure these diseases? Besides that, I am a poor man, in needy circumstances, and it is a help to me if I can make a little money with the sale of my books.

The Lord bless the beginning and the end of this little work, and be with us, that we may not misuse it, and thus commit a heavy sin!—The word misuse, means as much as to use it for anything unnecessary. God bless us! Amen. —The word amen means as much as that the Lord might bring to pass in reality what had been asked for in prayer.

HOHMAN.

ARTS & REMEDIES.

A good Remedy for Hysterics, (or Mother-Fits,) to be used three times.

Put that joint of the thumb which sits in the palm of the hand on the bare skin covering the small bone which stands out above the pit of the heart, and speak the following at the same time:

Matrix, patrix, lay thyself right and safe,
Or thou or I shall on the third day fill the grave. † † †

Another remedy for Hysterics, and for Colds.

This must be strictly attented to every evening, that is: whenever you pull off your shoes or stockings, run your finger in between all the toes, and smell it. This will certainly effect a cure.

A certain remedy to stop Bleeding-which cures, no matter how far a person be away, if only his first name is rightly pronounced while using it.
Jesus Christ, dearest blood!
That stoppeth the pain, and stoppeth the blood.

In this help you, *(first name)* God the Father, God the Son, God the Holy Ghost. Amen.

A remedy to be used when any one is falling away, and which has cured many persons.

Let the person in perfect soberness and without having conversed with any one, make water in a pot before sunrise; boil an egg in this urine, bore three small holes in this egg with a needle, and carry it to an ant-hill made by big ants; and the person will feel relieved as soon as the egg is devoured.

Another remedy to be applied when any one is sick; which has effected many a cure where doctors could not help.

Let the sick person, without having conversed with any one, make water in a bottle before sun-rise, close it up tight, and put it immediately in some box or chest, lock it and stop up the key-hole; the key must be carried in one of the pockets for three days, as nobody dare have it excepting the person who puts the bottle with urine in the chest or box.

A good remedy for Worms, to be used for men as well as for cattle.

Mary, God's Mother, traversed the land,
Holding three worms close in her hand;
One was white, the other was black, the third was red.

This must be repeated three times, at the same time stroking the person or animal with the hand; and at the end of each application strike the back of the person or the animal, to wit: at the first application once, at the second application twice, and at the third application three times; and then set the worms a certain time, but not less than 3 minutes.

A good remedy against Calumniation or Slander.

If you are calumniated or slandered to your very skin, to your very flesh, to your very bones, cast it back upon the false tongues. † † †

Take off your shirt, and turn it wrong side out, and then run your two thumbs along your body, close under the ribs, starting at the pit of the heart down to the thighs.

A good remedy for the Ferer.

Good morning, dear Thursday! Take away from (name) the 77-fold fevers! Oh! thou dear Lord Jesus Christ, take them away from him! † † †

This must be used on Thursday for the first time, on Friday for the second time, and on Saturday for the third time; and each time thrice. The prayer of faith has also to be said each time, and not a word dare be spoken to any one until the sun has risen. Neither dare the sick person speak to any one till after sunrise; nor eat pork, nor drink milk, nor cross a running water, for nine days.

A good remedy for the Colic.

I warn ye, ye colic fiends! There is one sitting in judgment, who speaketh: just or unjust. Therefore beware, ye colic fiends! † † †

To attach a Dog to a person, provided nothing else was used before to effect it.

Try to draw some of your blood, and let the dog eat it along with his food, and he will stay with you. Or scrape the four corners of your table while you are eating, and continue to eat with the same knife after having scraped the corners of the table. Let the dog eat those scrapings, and he will stay with you.

To make a Wand for searching for Iron, Ore, or Water.

On the first night of Christmas, between 11 & 12 o'clock, break off from any tree a young twig of one year's growth, in the three highest names, (Father, Son and Holy Ghost,) at the same time facing towards sunrise. Whenever you apply this wand in searching for anything, apply it three times. The twig must be forked, and each end of the fork must be held in one hand, so that the third and thickest part of it stands up, but do not hold it too tight. Strike the ground with the thickest end, and that which you desire will appear immediately, if there is any in the ground where you strike. The words to be spoken when the wand is thus applied, are as follows:

Archangel Gabriel, I conjure thee in the name of God, he Almighty, to tell me, is there any water here or not? tell me! † † †

If you search for iron or ore, you have to say the same, only mention the name of what you are searching for.

A very good remedy for Palpitation of the Heart, and for persons who are Hide-bound.

Palpitation and hide-bound, be off (name) ribs,
Since Christ, our Lord, spoke truth with his lips.

A Precaution against Injuries.

Whoever carries the right eye of a wolf fastened inside of his right sleeve, remains free from all injuries.

How to obtain things which are desired.

If you call upon another to ask for a favor, take care to carry a little of the firefinger-grass with you, and you shall certainly obtain that you desired.

A sure way of catching Fish.

Take rose seed and mustard seed, and the foot of a weasel, and hang these in a net, and the fish will certainly collect there.

A safe remedy for various ulcers, biles, and other defects.

Take the root of iron-weed, and tie it around the neck; it cures running ulcers; it also serves against obstructions in the bladder (stranguary,) and cures the piles, if the roots are boiled in water with honey, and drank; it cleans and heals the lungs and effects a good breath. If this root is planted among grape veins or fruit trees, it promotes the growth very much. Children who carry it, are educated without any difficulty; they become fond of all useful arts and sciences, and grow up joyfully and cheerfully.

A very good remedy for Mortification and Inflammation.

Sanctus Itorius res, call the rest. Here the Mother of God came to his assistance, reaching out her snow-white hand, against the hot and cold brand. † † †

Make three crosses with the thumb. Every thing which is applied in words, must be applied three times, and an interval of several hours must intervene each time, and for the third time it is to be applied the next day, unless where it is otherwise directed.

To prevent wicked or malicious persons from doing you an injury—against whom it is of great power.

Dullix, ix, ux. Yea, you can't come over Pontio; Pontio is above Pilato. † † †

A very good remedy to destroy Bots or Worms in Horses.

You must mention the name of the horse, and say: "If you have any worms, I will catch you by the forehead. If they be white, brown, or red, they shall and must now all be dead." You must shake the head of the horse three times, and pass your hand over his back three times to and fro. † † †

To cure the Pollevil in Horses, in two or three applications.

Break off 3 twigs from a cherry tree; one towards morning, one towards evening, and one towards midnight. Cut three small pieces off the hind part of your shirt, and wrap each of those twigs in one of these pieces; then clean the pollevil with the twigs, and lay them under the eaves. The ends of the twigs which had been in the wound must be turned towards the north; after which you must do your business on them, that is to say, you must s—t on them; then cover it, leaving the rags around the twigs. After all this the wound must again be stirred with the three twigs, in one or two days, and the twigs placed as before.

A good remedy for bad Wounds and Burns.

The word of God, the milk of Jesus' Mother, and Christ's blood, is for all wounds and burnings good. † † †

It is the safest way in all these cases to make the crosses with the hand or thumb three times over the affected parts; that is to say, over all those things to which the three crosses are attached.

A very good remedy for the Wild-fire.

Wild-fire and the dragon, flew over a wagon,
The wild-fire abated, and the dragon skeated.

To stop pains or smarting in a wound.

Cut three small twigs from a tree—each to be cut off in one cut—rub one end of each twig in the wound, and wrap them separately in a piece of white paper, and put them in a warm and dry place.

To destroy Warts.

Roast Chicken-feet and rub the warts with them, then bury them under the eaves.

To banish the Hooping Cough.

Cut three small bunches of hair from the crown of the head of a child that has never seen its father; sew this hair up in an unbleached rag and hang it around the neck of the child having the hooping cough. The thread with which the rag is sewed must also be unbleached.

Another remedy for the Hooping Cough, which has cured the majority of those who have applied it.

Thrust the child having the hooping-cough three times through a blackberry bush, without speaking or saying anything. The bush, however, must be grown fast at the two ends, and the child must be thrust through three times in the same manner, that is to say, from the same side it was thrust through in the first place.

A good remedy to stop Bleeding.

This is the day on which the injury happened. Blood, thou must stop, until the Virgin Mary bring forth another son.—Repeat these words three times.

To banish Convulsive Fevers.

Write the following letters on a piece of white paper, sew it in a piece of linen or muslin, and hang it around the neck until the fever leaves you:

A b a x a C a t a b a x
A b a x a C a t a b a x
A b a x a C a t a b a
A b a x a C a t a b
A b a x a C a t a
A b a x a C a t
A b a x a C a
A b a x a C
A b a x a
A b a x
A b a
A b
A

A good remedy for the Tooth-ache.

Stir the sore tooth with a needle until it draws blood; then take a thread and soak it with this blood. Then take vinegar and flower, mix them well so as to form a paste, and spread it on a rag, then wrap this rag around the root of an apple tree, and tie it very close with the above thread, after which the root must be well covered with ground.

How to banish the Fever.

Write the following words upon a paper and wrap it up in knot-grass, (breiten Wegrich,) and then tie it upon the navel of the person who has the fever:

Potmat sineat,
Potmat sineat,
Potmat sineat.

How to walk and step securely in all cases.

Jesus walketh with [name]. He is my head; I am his limb. Therefore walketh Jesus with [name]. † † †

A very good remedy for the Colic.

Take half a gill of good old rye whiskey, and a pipe full of tobacco; put the whiskey in a bottle, then smoke the tobacco and blow the smoke into the bottle, shake it up well and drink it. This has cured the author of this book, and many others.—Or take a white clay pipe which has turned blackish from smoking, pound it to a fine powder, and take it. This will have the same effect.

A very good Plaster.

I doubt very much whether any physician in the United States can make a plaster equal to this. It heals the white swelling, and has cured the sore leg of a woman who for 18 years had used the prescriptions of doctors in vain.

Take two quarts of cider, one pound of bees-wax, one pound of sheep-tallow, and one pound of tobacco; boil the tobacco in the cider till the strength is out, and then strain it and add the other articles to the liquid, stir it over a gentle fire till all is dissolved.

To make a good Eye Water.

Take four cents worth of white vitriol, four cents worth of prepared spicewort, (calamus root,) four cents worth of cloves, a gill of good whiskey, and a gill of water. Make the calamus fine, and mix all together; then use it after it has stood a few hours.

A very good remedy for the White-Swelling.

Take a quart of unslaked lime, and pour two quarts of water on it; stir it well and let it stand over night. The scum that collects on the lime water must be taken off, and a pint of flax-seed oil poured in, after which it must be stirred until it becomes somewhat consistent; then put it in a pot or pan, and add a little lard and wax, melt it well, and make a plaster, and apply it to the parts affected—the plaster should be renewed every day, or at least every other day until the swelling is gone.

A remedy for Epilepsy, provided the subject had never fallen into fire or water.

Write reversedly or backwards upon a piece of paper: "IT IS ALL OVER!" This is to be written but once upon the paper, then put it in a scarlet-red cloth, and then wrap it in a piece of unbleached linen, and hang it around the neck, on the first Friday of the new moon. The thread with which it is tied must also be unbleached. ☩ ☩ ☩

Remedy for Burns.

"Burn, I blow on thee!"—It must be blown on three times in the same breath, like the fire by the sun. † † †

To stop Bleeding.

Count backwards from fifty inclusive till you come down to three. As soon as you arrive at three, you will be done bleeding.

A remedy to relieve Pain.

Take a rag which was tied over a wound for the first time, and put it in water together with some copperas; but do not venture to stir the copperas until you are certain of the pain having left you.

A good remedy for the Tooth-ache.

Cut out a piece of greensword (sod) in the morning before sunrise, quite unbeshrewedly, from any place, breathe three times upon it, and put it down upon the same place from which it was taken.

To remove Bruises and Pains.

Bruise, thou shalt not heat;
Bruise, thou shalt not sweat;
Bruise, thou shalt not run,
No more than Virgin Mary shall bring forth another son. † † †

A remarkable passage from the book of Albertus Magnus.

It says: If you burn a large frog to ashes and mix the ashes with water, you will obtain an ointment that will, if put on any place covered with hair, destroy the hair and prevent it from growing again.

Another passage from the work of Alburtus Magnus.

If you find the stone which a vulture has in his knees, and which you may find by looking sharp, and put it in the vituals of two persons who hate each other, it causes them to make up and be good friends.

To cure Fits or Convulsions.

You must go upon another person's land, and repeat the following words: "I go before another court—I tie up my 77-fold fits." Then cut three small twigs off any tree on the land, in each twig you must make a knot. This must be done on a Friday morning before sunrise, in the decrease of the moon, unbeshrewedly. † † † Then over your body where you feel the fits you make the crosses.—And thus they must be made in all cases where they are applied.

Cure for the Head-ache.

Tame thou flesh and bone, like Christ in Paradise; and who will assist thee, this I tell thee, (name,) for your repentance-sake. † † † This you must say three times, each time pausing for three minutes, and your head-ache will soon cease. But if your head-ache is caused by strong drink, or otherwise will not leave you soon, then you must repeat those words every minute. This, however, is not often necessary in regard to head-ache.

To mend Broken Glass.

Take common cheese and wash it well, unslaked lime and the white of eggs, rub all these well together until it becomes one mass, and then use it. If it is made right, it will certainly hold.

How to make Cattle return to the same place.

Pull out three small bunches of hair, one between the horns, one from the middle of the back, and one near the tail, and make your cattle eat it in their feed.

Another method of making Cattle return home.

Take a handful of salt, go upon your fields and make your cattle walk three times around the same. stump or stone, each time keeping the same direction, that is to say, you must three times arrive at the same end of the stump or stone at which your started from, and then let your cattle lick the salt from the stump or stone.

To prevent the Hessian Fly from Injuring the Wheat.

Take pulverised charcoal, make ley of it, and soak the seed-wheat in it; take it out of the ley, and on every bushel of wheat sprinkle a quart of urine; stir it well, then spread it out to dry.

To prevent Cherries from ripening before Martinmas.

Engraft the twigs upon a mulberry tree, and your desire is accomplished.

Stinging Nettle—good for banishing fears and fancies, and to cause fish to collect.

Whenever you hold this weed in your hand together with Millifolia, you are safe from all fears and fancies that frequently deceive men. If you mix it with a decoction of the hemlock, and rub your hands with it, and put the rest in water that contains fish, you will find the fish to collect around your hands. Whenever you pull your hands out of the water, the fish disappear by returning to their former places.

Heliotrope, (sun-flower)—*a means to prevent Calumniation.*

The virtues of this plant is miraculous, if it be collected in the sign of the lion, in the month of August, and wrapped up in a laurel leaf, together with the tooth of a wolf. Whoever carries this about him, will never be addressed harshly by any one, but all will speak to him kindly and peaceably. And if any thing has been stolen from you, put this under your head during the night, and you will surely see the whole figure of the thief. This has been found true.

To heal a Sore Mouth.

If you have the scurvy, or quinsey too,
I breathe my breath three times into you.
✝ ✝ ✝

Swallow-wort,

A means to overcome and end all fighting and anger, and to cause a sick man to weep when his health is restored, or to sing with a cheerful voice when on his death-bed; also a very good remedy for dim eyes, or shining of the eyes.—This weed grows at the time when the swallows built their nests, or eagles breed. If a man carries this about him, together with the heart of a mole, he shall overcome all fighting and anger. If these things are put upon the head of a sick man, he shall weep at the restoration of his health, and sing with a cheerful voice when he comes to die. When the swallow-wort blooms, the flowers must be pounded up and boiled, and then the water must be poured off into another vessel, and again be placed to the fire and carefully skimmed; then it must be filtered through a cloth and preserved, and whosoever has dim eyes, or shining eyes, may bathe his eyes with it, and they will become clear and sound.

A good remedy for Consumption.

Consumption, I order thee out of the bones into the flesh, out of the flesh upon the skin, out of the skin into the wilds of the forest. ✝ ✝ ✝

For the Hollow Horn in Cows.

Bore a small hole in the hollow horn, milk the same cow, and squirt her milk in the horn; this is the best cure. Use a syringe to squirt the milk into the horn.

A very good and certain means of destroying the Wheal in the Eye.

Take a dirty plate, if you have none, you can easily dirty one, and the person for whom you are using sympathy shall in a few minutes find the pain much relieved. You must hold that side of the plate or dish, which is used in eating, towards the eye. While you hold the plate before your eye, you must say:

Dirty plate I press thee,
Wheal in the eye do flee.
† † †

To make Chickens lay many Eggs.

Take the dung of rabbits, pound it to powder, mix it with bran, wet the mixture till it forms lumps, and feed your chickens with it, and they will keep on laying a great many eggs.

Words to be spoken while making Divinatory Wands.

In making divinatory wands, they must be broken as before directed, and while breaking and before using them, the following words must be spoken:

Divining wand, do thou keep that power,
Which God gave unto thee at the very first hour.

How to destroy a Tape Worm.

Worm, I conjure thee by the living God, that thou shalt flee this blood and this flesh, like as God the Lord will flee that judge who judges unjustly, although he might have judged aright. † † †

A good remedy for the Bots in Horses.

Every time you use this, you must stroke the horse down with the hand three times, and lead it about three times, holding its head towards the sun, saying: "The Holy One sayeth: Joseph passed over a field and there he found three small worms; the one being black, another being brown, and the third being red; thus thou shalt die and be dead."

How to cure a Burn.

Three holy men went out walking,
They did bless the heat and the burning;
They blessed that it might not increase;
They blessed that it might quickly cease!
† † †

To cure the Bite of a Snake.

God has created all things, and they were good;
Thou only, serpent, art damned,
Cursed be thou and thy sting.
† † †

Zing, zing, zing!

Security against Mad Dogs.

Dog, hold thy nose to the ground,
God has made me and thee, hound!
† † †

This you must repeat in the direction of the dog; and the three crosses you must make towards the dog, and the words must be spoken before he sees you.

To remove Pain and heal up Wounds with Three Switches.

With this switch and Christ's dear blood,
I banish your pain and do you good!
† † †

Mind it well you must in one cut, sever from a tree, a young branch pointing towards sunrise, and then make three pieces of it, which you successively put in the wound. Holding them in your hand, you take the one towards your right side first. — Every thing prescribed in this book must be used three times, even if the three crosses should not be affixed. Words are always to have an interval of half an hour, and between the second and third time should pass a whole night, except where it is otherwise directed. The above three sticks, after the end of each has been put into the wound as before directed, must be put in a piece of white paper, and placed where they will be warm and dry.

Remedy for Fever, Worms, and the Colic.

Jerusalem, thou Jewish city,
In which Christ, our Lord, was born,
Thou shalt turn into water and blood,
Because it is for (name,) fever, worms, and colic good.
† † †

How to cure Weakness of the Limbs.

Take the buds of the birch tree, or the inner bark of the root of the tree at the time of the budding of the birch, and make a tea of it, and drink it occasionally through the day. Yet after having used it for two weeks, it must be discontinued for a while, before it is resorted to again; and during the two weeks of its use, it is well at times to use water for a day, instead of the tea.

Another remedy for Weakness.

Take Bittany and St. John's-wort, and put them in good old rye whiskey. To drink some of this in the morning before having taken any thing else, is very wholesome and good. A tea made of the acorns of the white oak is also very good for weakness of the limbs.

A good method of destroying Rats and Mice.

Every time you bring grain into your barn, you must, in putting down the three first sheaves, repeat the following words: "Rats and mice, these three sheaves I give to you, in order that you may not destroy any of my wheat." The name of the kind of grain must always be mentioned.

To make Horses that refuse their Feed to eat again—especially applicable when they are afflicted in this manner on the public roads.

Open the jaws of the horse, which refuses his feed, and knock three times on his palate. This will certainly cause the horse to eat again without hesitation, and to go along willingly.

To cure any Excrescence or Wen on a Horse.

Take any bone which you accidently find, for you dare not be looking for it, and rub the wen of the horse with it; always bearing in mind that it must be done in the decreasing moon, and the wen will certainly disappear. The bone, however, must be replaced as it was laying before.

How to prepare a good Eye-Water.

Take one ounce of white vitriol and one ounce of sugar of lead, dissolve them in oil of rosemary, and put it in a quart bottle, which you fill up with rose water. Bathe the eyes with it night and morning.

How to cause male or female thieves to stand still, without being able to move backward or forward.

In using any prescriptions of this book in regard to making others stand still, it is best to be walking about; and repeat the following three times:

"Oh Peter, oh Peter, borrow the power from God: what I shall bind with the bands of a christian hand, shall be bound; all male or female thieves, be they great or small, young or old, shall be spell-bound by the power of God, and not be able to walk forward or backward, until I see them with my eyes, and give them leave with my tongue, except it be that they count for me all the stones that may be between heaven and earth, all rain-drops, all the leaves and all the grass in the world. This I pray for the repentance of my enemies." † † † Repeat your articles of faith and the Lord's prayer.

If the thieves are to remain alive, the sun dare not shine upon them before their release. There are two ways of releasing them, which will be particularly stated: The first is this, that you tell him in the name of St. John to leave: the other is as follows: "The words which have bound thee, shall give thee free." † † †

To cure the Sweeney in Horses.

Take a piece of old bacon, and cut it into small pieces, put them in a pan and roast them well, put in a handful of fish-worms, a gill of oats, and three spoonsful of salt into it; roast the whole of this until it turns black, and then filter it through a cloth; after which you put a gill of soft soap, half a gill of rye whiskey, half a gill of vinegar, and half a gill of the urine of a boy to it; mix it well, and smear it over the part affected with sweeney, on the third, the sixth, and the ninth day of the new moon, and warm it with an oaken board.

How to make Molasses.

Take pumpkins, boil them, press the juice out of them, and boil the juice to a proper consistence. There is nothing else necessary. The author of this book, John George Hohman, has tasted this molasses, thinking it was the genuine kind, until the people of the house told him what it was.

To make good Beer.

Take a handful of hops, five or six gallons of water, about three table-spoonsful of ginger, half a gallon of molasses; filter the water, hops and ginger into a tub containing the molasses.

Cure for the Epilepsy.

Take a turtle-dove, cut its throat, and let the person afflicted with epilepsy drink the blood.

Another way to make Cattle return home.

Feed your cattle out of a pot or kettle used in preparing your dinner, and they will always return to your stable.

A very good remedy to cure Sores.

Boil the bulbs (roots) of the white lilly in cream, and put it on the sore in form of a plaster. Southernwort has the same effect.

A good cure for Wounds.

Take the bones of a calf, and burn them until they turn power, and then strew it into the wound. This powder prevents the flesh from putrifying, and is therefore of great importance in healing the wound.

To make an Oil out of Paper, which is good for sore eyes.

A man from Germany informed me, that to burn two sheets of white paper would produce about three drops of oil or water, which would heal all sores in or about the eye if rubbed with it. Any affection of the eyes can be cured in this way, as long as the apple of the eye is sound.

To destroy Crab-Lice.

Take capuchin powder, mix it with hog's lard, and smear yourself with it. Or, boil cammock, and wash the place where the lice keep themselves.

To prevent the worst kind of paper from blotting.

Dissolve alum in water, and put it on the paper, and I, Hohman, would like to see who cannot write on it, after it is dried.

A very good remedy for the Gravel.

The author of this book, John George Hohman, applied this remedy, and soon felt relieved. I knew a man who could find no relief from the medicine of any doctor; he then used the following remedy, to wit: he eat every morning seven peach stones before tasting anything else, which relieved him very much; but as he had the gravel very bad, he was obliged to use it constantly. I, Hohman, have used it for several weeks. I still feel a touch of it now and then, yet I had it so badly that I cried out aloud every time I had to make water. I owe a thousand thanks to God and the person who told me of this remedy.

A good remedy for those who cannot keep their water.

Burn a hog's bladder to powder, and take it inwardly.

To destroy Field-Mice and Moles.

Put unslaked lime in their holes, and they will disappear.

To remove a Wen during the crescent moon.

Look over the wen directly towards the moon, and say: "Whatever grows, does grow; and what diminishes, does diminish." This must be said three times in the same breath.

To remove a Scum or Skin from the Eye.

Before sunrise on St. Bartholomew's day, you must dig up four or five roots of the dandelion weed, taking good care to get the ends of the roots; then you must procure a rag and a thread that have never been in the water; the thread, which dare not have a single knot in it, is used in sewing up the roots into the rag, and the whole is then to be hanged before the eye until the scum disappears. The tape by which it it is fastened, must never have been in the water.

For deafness, roaring or buzzing in the ear, & for tooth-ache.

A few drops of refined camphor-oil put upon cotton, and thus applied to the aching tooth, relieves very much. When put in the ear, it strengthens the hearing, and removes the roaring and whizzing in the same.

A good way to cause children to cut their teeth without pain.

Boil the brain of a rabbit, and rub the gums of the children with it, and their teeth will grow without any pain to them.

For Vomiting and Diarrhoea.

Take pulverised cloves and eat them together with bread soaked in red wine, and you will soon find relief. The cloves may be put upon the bread.

To Heal Burns.

Pound or press the juice out of male fern, and put it on the burnt spots, and they will heal very fast. Better yet, however, if you smear the above juice upon a rag, and put that on like a plaster.

A very good cure for weakness of the limbs, for the purification of the blood, for the invigoration of the head & heart, and to remove giddiness, &c. &c.

Take two drops of the oil of cloves in a table-spoonful of white wine, early in the morning, and before eating anything else. This is also good for the mother-pains, and the colic. The oil of cloves which you buy in the drug stores will answer the purpose. These remedies are also applicable to cure the cold when it settles in the bowels, and to stop vomiting. A few drops of this oil poured upon cotton and applied to the aching teeth, relieves the pain.

For Dysentery and Diarrhoea.

Take the moss off of trees, and boil it in red wine, and let those that are affected with these diseases, drink it.

Cure for the Tooth-Ache.

Hohman, the author of this book, has cured the severest tooth-ache more than sixty times, with this remedy; and out of the sixty times he applied it, it failed but once in affecting a cure. Take blue vitriol and put a small piece of it in the hollow tooth, yet not too much; spit out the water that collects in the mouth, and be careful to swallow none. I do not know whether it is good for teeth that are not hollow, but I should judge it would cure any kind of toothache.

Advise to Pregnant Women.

Pregnant women must be very careful not to use any camphor; and no camphor should be administered to those women who have the mother-fits.

Cure for the Bite of a Mad Dog.

A certain Mr. Valentine Kettering, of Dauphin County, has communicated to the Senate of Pennsylvania, a sure remedy for the bite of any kind of mad animals. He says that his ancestors had already used it in Germany 250 years ago, and that he had always found it to answer the purpose, during a residence of fifty years in the United States. He only published it from motives of humanity. This remedy consists in the weed called *Chick-weed*. It is a summer plant, known to the Germans and Swiss by the names of *Gauchneil, Rother Meyer,* or *Rother Huehnerdarm*. In England it is called *Red Pimpernel,* and its botanical name is *Angelica Phonicea*. It must be gathered in June, when in full bloom, and dried in the shade, and then pulverized.—The dose of this for a grown person, is a small table-spoonful, or in weight a drachm and a scruple, at once, in beer or water. For children the dose is the same, yet it must be administered at three different times. In applying it to animals, it must be used green, cut to pieces, and mixed with bran or other feed. For hogs, the pulverised weed is made into little balls by mixing it with flower and water. It can also be put on bread and butter, or in honey, molasses, &c.—The Rev. Henry Muhlenberg says, that in Germany 30 grains of the powder of this weed are given four times a day, the first day, then one dose a day for a whole week ; while, at the same time, the wound is washed out with a decoction of the weed, and then the powder strewed in it.—Mr. Kettering says that he in all instances administered but one dose, with the most happy results. This is said to be the same remedy through which the late Doctor William Stoy effected so many cures.

A very good means to increase the growth of Wool on Sheep, and to prevent disease among them.

William Ellis, in his excellent work on the English manner of raising sheep, relates the following: I knew a tenant who had a flock of sheep that produced an unusual quantity of wool. He informed me, that he was in the habit of washing his sheep with butter-milk just after shearing them, which was the cause of the unusual growth of wool; because it is a known fact that buttermilk does not only improve the growth of sheep's wool, but also of the hair of other animals. Those who have no butter-milk may substitute common milk, mixed with salt and water, which will answer nearly as well to wash the sheep just sheared. And I guarantee that by rightly applying this means, you will not only have a great increase of wool, but the sheep-lice and their entire brood will be destroyed. It also cures all manner of scab and itch, and prevents the sheep from catching cold.

A well-tried Plaster to remove Mortification.

Take six hen eggs and boil them in hot ashes until they are right hard, then take the yellow of the eggs and fry them in a gill of lard until they are quite black, then put a handful of rue with it, and afterwards filter it through a cloth. When this is done, add a gill of sweet oil to it. It will take most effect where the plaster for a female is prepared by a male, and the plaster for a male prepared by a female.

A good remedy for the Poll-Evil in Horses.

Take white turpentine, rub it over the poll-evil with your hand, and then melt it with a hot iron so that it runs into the wound. After this, take neatsfoot oil or goose grease, and rub it into the wound in the same manner, and for three days in succession, commencing on the last Friday of the last quarter of the moon.

For the Scurvy and Sore Throat.

Speak the following, and it will certainly help you: Job went through the land, holding his staff close in the hand, when God the Lord did meet him, and said to him: Job, what art thou grieved at? Job said: Oh God, why should I not be sad? My throat and my mouth are rotting away. Then said the Lord to Job: In yonder valley there is a well, which will cure thee, [name] and thy mouth, and thy throat, in the name of God the Father, the Son, and the Holy Ghost. Amen.

This must be spoken three times in the morning, and three times in the evening; and where it reads "which will cure," you must blow three times in the child's mouth.

A very good Plaster.

Take wormwood, rue, medels, sheepripwort, pointy plantain, in equal proportions, a larger proportion of beeswax and tallow, and some spirits of turpentine, put it together in a pot, boil it well, and then strain it, and you have a very good plaster.

To stop Bleeding.
I walk through a green forest;
There I find three wells, cool and cold;
The first is called courage,
The second is called good,
And the third is called, stop the blood.
† † †

Another way to stop Bleeding, and to heal Wounds, in man as well as animals.

On Christ's grave there grows three roses; the first is kind, the second is valued among the rulers, and the third says: blood thou must stop, and wound thou must heal.—Every thing prescribed for man in this book, is also applicable to animals.

For gaining a Lawful Suit.

It reads, if any one has to settle any just claim by way of a law suit, let him take some of the largest kind of sage and write the names of the 12 apostles on the leaves, and put them in his shoes before entering the courthouse, and he shall certainly gain the suit.

For the Swelling of Cattle.

To Desh break no Flesh, but to Desh! While saying this run your hand along the back of the animal. † † †

Note—The hand must be put upon the bare skin in all cases of using sympathetic words.

An easy method of Catching Fish.

In a vessel of white glass must be put: 8 grains of civit, (musk) and as much castorium; 2 ounces of eel-fat, and 4 ounces of unsalted butter; after which the vessel must be well closed, and put in some place where it will keep moderately warm, for nine or ten days, and then the composition must be well stirred with a stick until it is perfectly mixed.

Application.—

1. *In using the hooks*—Worms or insects used for baiting the hooks, must first be moistened with this composition, and then put in a bladder or box, which may be carried in the pocket.
2. *In using the net*—Small balls formed of the soft part of fresh bread must be dipped in this composition, and then by means of thread fastened inside of the net before throwing it into the water.
3. *Catching fish with the hand*—Besmear your legs or boots with this composition before entering the water, at the place where the fish are expected, and they will collect in great numbers around you.

A very good and safe Remedy for Rheumatism.

From one to two dollars have often been paid for this recipe alone, it being the best and surest remedy to cure the rheumatism. Let it be known therefore: Take a piece of cloth, some tape and thread, neither of which must ever have been in water; the thread must not have a single knot in it, and the cloth and tape must have been spun by a child not quite or at least not more than seven years of age. The letter given below must be carefully sowed in the piece of cloth, and tied around the neck, unbeshrewedly, on the first Friday in the decreasing moon; and immediately after hanging it around the neck, the Lord's prayer and the articles of faith must be repeated. What now follows must be written in the before mentioned letter:

"May God the Father, Son, and Holy Ghost grant it, Amen. Seek immediately, and seek; thus commandeth the Lord thy God, through the first man whom God did love upon earth. Seek immediately, and seek; thus commandeth the Lord thy God, through Luke, the Evangelist, and through Paul, the Apostle. Seek immediately, and seek; thus commandeth the Lord thy God, through the twelve messengers. Seek immediately, and seek; thus commandeth the Lord thy God, by the first man, that God might be loved. Seek immediately, and convulse; thus commandeth the Lord thy God, through the Holy Fathers, who have been made by divine and holy writ. Seek immediately, and convulse; thus commandeth the Lord thy God, through the dear and holy angels, and through his paternal and divine Omnipotence, and his heavenly confidence and endurance. Seek immediately, and convulse; thus commandeth the Lord thy God, through the burning oven which was preserved by the blessing of God. Seek immediately, and convulse; thus commandeth the Lord thy God, through all power and might, through the prophet Jonah who was preserved in the belly of the whale for three days and three nights, by the blessing of God. Seek immediately, and convulse; thus commandeth the Lord thy God, through all the power and might which proceed from divine humility, and in all eternity; whereby no harm be done unto † N † nor unto any part of his body, be they the raving convulsions, or the yellow convulsions, or the white convulsions, or the red convulsions, or the black convulsions, or by whatever name convulsions may be called; these all shall do no harm unto thee † N † nor to any part of thy body, nor to thy head, nor to thy neck, nor to thy heart, nor to thy stomach, nor to any of thy reins, nor to thy arms, nor to thy legs, nor to thy eyes, nor to thy tongue, nor to any part or parcel of thy body. This I write for thee † N † in these words, and in the name of God the Father, the Son, and the Holy Ghost, Amen.—God bless it. Amen."

Note.—If any one writes such a letter for another, the Christian name of the person must be mentioned in it; as you will observe, where the N stands singly in the above letter, there must be the name.

A good way to destroy Worms in Bee-Hives.

With very little trouble and at an expense of a quarter dollar, you can certainly free your bee-hives from worms for a whole year. Get from an apothecary store the powder called Pensses Blum, which will not injure the bees in the least. The application of it is as follows: For one beehive you take as much of this powder, as the point of your knife will hold, mix it with one ounce of good whiskey, and put it in a common vial, then make a hole in the bee-hive and pour it in thus mixed with the whiskey, which is sufficient for one hive at once. Make the hole so that it can be easily poured in. As said before, a quarter dollar's worth of this powder is enough for one hive.

Recipe for making a paste to prevent gun barrels from rusting, whether iron or steel.

Take one ounce of bear's fat, half an ounce of badger-grease, half an ounce of snake's fat, one ounce of almond oil, and a quarter of an ounce of pulverized indigo, and melt it all together in a new vessel over a fire, stir it well, and put it afterwards into some vessel. In using it, a lump as large as a common nut must be put upon a piece of woolen cloth and then rubbed on the barrel and lock of the gun, and it will keep the barrel from rusting.

To make a Wick which is never consumed.

Take an ounce of asbestos and boil it in a quart of strong ley for two hours; then pour off the ley and clarify what remains by pouring rain water on it three or four times, after which you can form a wick from it which will never be consumed by the fire.

A Morning Prayer, to be spoken before starting on a journey, which will save the person from all mishaps.

I, [here the name is to be pronounced,] will go on a journey to-day; I will walk upon God's way, and walk where God himself did walk, and our dear Lord Jesus Christ, and our dearest Virgin with her dear little babe, with her seven rings and her true things. Oh thou! my dear Lord Jesus Christ, I am thine own, that no dog may bite me, no wolf bite me, and no murderer secretly approach me: Save me, oh my God, from sudden death! I am in God's hands, and there I will bind myself. In God's hands I am by our

Lord Jesus' five wounds, that any gun or other arms may not do me any more harm than the virginity of our Holy Virgin Mary was injured by the favour of her beloved Jesus.—After this say three Lord's prayer, the Ava Maria, and the articles of faith.

A safe and approved means to be applied in times of Fire and Pestilence.

Wellcome! thou firey fiend! do not extend further than thou already hast. This I count unto thee as a repentant act, in the name of God the Father, the Son, and the Holy Ghost.

I command unto thee, fire, by the power of God, which createth and worketh every thing, that thou now do cease, and not extend any further; as certainly as Christ was standing on the Jordan's stormy banks being baptised by John, the holy man.

This I count unto thee as a repentant act, in the name of the holy Trinity.

I command unto thee, fire, by the power of God, now to abate thy flames; as certainly as Mary retained her virginity before all ladies who retained theirs, so chaste and pure; therefore, fire, cease thy wrath.

This I count unto thee, fire, as a repentant act, in the name of the most holy trinity.

I command unto thee, fire, to abate thy heat, by the precious blood of Jesus Christ, which he has shed for us, and our sins and transgressions.

This I count unto thee, fire, as a repentant act, in the name of God the Father, the Son, and the Holy Ghost. Jesus of Nazareth, a king of the Jews, help us from this dangerous fire, and guard this land and its bounds from al! epidemic disease and pestilence.

REMARKS.

This has been discovered by a christian Gipsey King of Egypt —Anno 1740, on the 10th of June, six Gipsies were executed on the gallows in the Kingdom of Prussia. The seventh of their party was a man of eighty years of age, and was to be executed by the sword, on the 16th of the same month. But fortunately for him, quite unexpectedly a conflagration broke out, and the old Gipsey was taken to the fire to try his arts; which he successfully done to the great surprise of all present, by bespeaking the conflagration in a manner that it wholly and entirely ceased and disappeared in less than ten minutes. Upon this, the proof having been given in day time, he received pardon and was set at liberty. This was confirmed and attested by the government of the King of Prussia, and the General Superintendent at Koenigsberg, and given to the public in print. It was first published at Koenigsberg in Prussia, by Alexander Bausman, anno 1745.

Whoever has this epistle in his house, will be safe from all danger of fire, as well as from lightning. If a pregnant. woman carries this letter about her, neither enchantment or evil spirits can injure her or her child. Further, if any body has this letter in his house, or carries it about his person, he will be safe from the injuries of pestilence.

While saying these sentences one must pass three times around the fire. This has availed in all instances.

To prevent Conflagration.

Take a black chicken in the morning or evening, cut its head off and throw it upon the ground; cut its stomach out, yet leave it all together; then try to get a piece of a shirt which was worn by a chaste virgin during her terms, and cut out a piece as large as a common dish from that part which is bloodiest. These two things wrap up together, then try to get an egg which was laid on maunday Thursday. These three things put together in wax; then put them in a pot holding eight quarts, and bury it under the threshhold of your house, with the aid of God, and as long as there remains a single stick of your house together, no conflagration will happen.—If your house should happen to be on fire already in front and behind, the fire will, nevertheless, do no injury to you, nor to your children. This is done by the power of God, and is quite certain and infallible.—If fire should break out unexpectedly, then try to get a whole shirt in which your servant maid had her terms, or a sheet on which a child was born, and throw it into the fire, wrapped up in a bundle, and without saying anything. This will certainly stop it.

To prevent Witches from bewitching Cuttle, to be written and placed in the stable; and against Bad Men and Evil Spirits, which nightly torment old and young people, to be written and placed on the bedstead.

"Trotter Head, I forbid thee my house and premises, forbid thee my horse and cow stable, I forbid thee my bedstead, that thou mayest not breathe upon me: breathe into some other house, until thou hast ascended every hill, until thou hast counted every fence post, and until thou hast crossed every water And thus dear day may come again into my house, in the name of God the Father, the Son, and the Holy Ghost. Amen."

This will certainly protect and free all persons and animals from witchcraft.

To prevent bad people from getting about the Cattle.

Take wormwood, gith, five-finger weed, and assafoedita; three cents worth of each; the straw of horse-beans, some dirt swept together behind the door of the stable, and a little salt. Tie these all up together with a tape, and put the bundle in a hole about the threshold over which your cattle pass in and out, and cover it well with lignum vitæ wood. This will certainly be of use.

To Extinguish Fire without later.

Write the following letters upon each side of a plate, and throw it into the fire, and it will be extinguished forthwith:

$$
\begin{matrix}
S & A & T & O & R \\
A & R & E & P & O \\
T & E & N & E & T \\
O & P & E & R & A \\
R & O & T & A & S \\
\end{matrix}
$$

Another Method of stopping Fire.

Our Dear Sarah journeyeth through the land, having a firy, hot brand in her hand. The firy brand heats; the firy brand sweats. Firy brand stop your heat; firy brand stop your sweat.

How to Fasten or Spell-bind anything.

You say: "Christ's cross and Christ's crown, Christ Jesus' coloured blood, be thou every hour good. God, the Father, is before me; God, the Son, is beside me ; God, the Holy Ghost, is behind me. Whoever now is stronger than these three persons, may come by day or night, to attack me." † † † Then say the Lord's prayer three times.

Another way of Fastening or Spell-binding.

After repeating the above, you speak: "At every step may Jesus walk with [name]. He is my head, I am his limb; therefore Jesus be with [name].

A Benediction to prevent Fire.

"The bitter sorrows and the death of our dear Lord Jesus Christ shall prevail: Fire, and wind, and great heat, and all that is within the power of these elements, I command thee through the Lord Jesus Christ, who has spoken to the winds and the waters, and they obeyed him. By these powerful words spoken by Jesus, I command, threaten, and inform thee, fire, flame, and heat, and your powers as elements, to flee forthwith. The holy, rosy blood of our dear Lord Jesus Christ, may rule it. Thou, fire and wind, and great heat, I command thee, as the Lord did by his holy angels command the great heat in the firy oven when those three holy men, Sadrach and his companions, Mesach and Obed Rego, to leave them untouched, as was done accordingly. Thus they shalt abate, thou fire, flame, and great heat, the Almighty God having spoken in creating the four elements, together with heaven and earth: Fiat, Fiat, Fiat! that is It shall be, in the name of God, the Father, the Son, and the Holy Ghost. Amen."

How to Relieve Persons or Animals after being Bewitched.

Three false tongues have bound thee, three holy tongues have spoken for thee. The first is God, the father, the second is God, the son, and the third is God, the holy ghost. They will give you blood and flesh, peace and comfort.—Flesh and blood are grown upon thee, born on thee, and lost on thee. If any man trample on thee with his horse, God will bless thee, and the holy Ciprian; has any woman trampled on thee, God and the body of Mary shall bless thee; if any servant has given you trouble, I bless thee through God and the laws of heaven; if any servant maid or woman has led you astray, God and the heavenly constellations shall bless thee. Heaven is above thee, the earth is beneath thee, and thou art between. I bless thee against all tramplings by horses. Our dear Lord Jesus Christ walked about in his bitter afflictions and death; and all the Jews that had spoken and promised, trembled in their falsehoods and mockery. Look, now trembleth the Son of God, as if he had the itch, said the Jews. And then spake Jesus: I have not the itch, and no one shall have it. Whoever will assist me to carry the cross, him I will free from the itch, in the name of God, the father, the son, and the holy ghost. Amen.

To protect houses and premises against Sickness & Theft.

Ito, alo Massa Dandi Bando, III. Amen. J. R. N. R. J.

Our Lord Jesus Christ stepped into the hall, and the Jews searched him everywhere. Thus shall those who now speak evil of me with their false tongues, and contend against me, one day bear sorrows, be silenced, dumbstruck, intimidated, and abused, for ever and ever, by the glory of

God. The glory of God shall assist me in this. Do thou aid me J. J. J. for ever and ever. Amen.

Against Mishaps and Dangers in the house.

Sanct Matheus, Sanct Marcus, Sanct Lucas, Sanct Johannis.

A Direction for a Gipsy-Sentence, to be carried about the person, as a protection under all circumstances.

Like unto the prophet Jonas, as a type of Christ, who was guarded for three days and three nights in the belly of a whale, thus shall the Almighty God, as a father, guard and protect me from all evil. J. J. J.

Against Evil Spirits and all manner of Witchcraft.

I.
N. I. R.
I.
SANCTUS SPIRITUS.
I.
N. I. R.
I.

All this be guarded, here in time, and there in eternity. Amen.

You must write all the above on a piece of white paper, and carry it about you. — The characters or letters above, signify: "God bless me here in time, and there eternally."

Against Swellings.

"Three pure Virgins went out on a journey, to inspect a swelling and sickness. The first one said: It is hoarse. The second said: It is not. The third said: If it is not, then will our Lord Jesus Christ come." This must be spoken in the name of the Holy Trinity.

Against Adversities and all manner of Contentions.

Power, hero, Prince of Peace, J. J. J.

Against Danger and Death, to be carried about the person.

I know that my Redeemer liveth, and that he will call me from the grave, &c.

How to Treat a Cow after the Milk is taken from her.

Give to the cow three spoonsful of her last milk, and say to the spirits in her blood: Ninny has done it, and I have swallowed her in the name of God, the father, the son, and the holy ghost. Amen."—Pray what you choose at the same time.

Another method of treating a Sick Cow.

J. The cross of Jesus Christ poured out milk;
J. The cross of Jesus Christ poured out water;
J. The cross of Jesus Christ has poured them out.

These lines must be written on three pieces of white paper, then take the milk of the sick cow and these three pieces of paper, put them in a pot, and scrape a little of the scull of a criminal on them; close it well, and put it over a hot fire, and the witch will have to die.—If you take the three pieces of paper, with the writing on them, in your mouth, and go out before your house, speak three times, and then give them to your cattle, you shall not only see all the witches, but your cattle will also get well again.

Against the Fever.

Pray early in the morning, and then turn your shirt around the left sleeve, and say: "turn thou, shirt, and thou, fever, do likewise, turn. [Do not forget to mention the name of the person having the fever.] This I tell thee, for thy repentance sake, in the name of God, the father, the son, and the holy ghost. Amen.—If you repeat this for three successive mornings, the fever will disappear.

To Spell-bind a Thief so that he cannot stir.

This benediction must be spoken a Thursday morning, before sunrise, and in the open air:

"Thus shall rule it God, the father, the son, and the holy ghost, Amen. Thirty-three Angels speak to each other, coming to administer in company with Mary. Then spoke dear Daniel, the holy one: Trust, my dear woman, I see some thieves coming who intend stealing your dear babe; this I cannot conceal from you. Then spake our dear lady to Saint Peter: I have bound with a band, through Christ's hand; therefore my thieves are bound even by the hand of Christ, if they wish to steal mine own, in the house, in the chest, upon the meadow or fields, in the woods, in the orchard, in the vineyard, or in the garden, or wherever they intend to steal. Our dear lady said: Whoever chooses may steal; yet if any one does steal, he shall stand like a buck, he shall stand like a stake, and shall count all the stones upon the earth, and all the stars in the heavens. Thus I give thee leave, and command every spirit to be master over every thief, by the guardianship of Saint Daniel, and by the burden of this world's goods. And the countenance shall be unto thee, that thou canst not move from the spot, as long as my tongue in the flesh shall not give thee leave. This I command thee by the holy virgin Mary, the Mother of God, by the power and might by which he has created heaven and earth, by the host of all the angels, and by all the Saints of God, the father, the son, and the holy ghost, Amen."—If you wish to set the thief free, you must tell him to leave in the name of Saint John.

Another way to Still-bind Thieves.

Ye thieves, I conjure you, to be obedient like Jesus Christ, who obeyed his heavenly father unto the cross, and to stand without moving out of my sight, in the name of the Trinity. I command you by the power of God and the incarnation of Jesus Christ, not to move out of my sight, † † † like Jesus Christ was standing on Jordan's stormy banks to be baptized by John. And furthermore, I conjure you, horse and rider, to stand still and not to move out of my sight, like Jesus Christ did stand when he was about to be nailed to the cross to release the fathers of the church from the bonds of hell. Ye thieves, I bind you with the same bonds with which Jesus our Lord has bound hell; and thus ye shall be bound; † † † and the same words that bind you, shall also release you.

To effect the same in less time.

Thou horseman and footman, you are coming under your hats; you are scattered! With the blood of Jesus Christ, with his five holy wounds, thy barrel, thy gun, and thy pistol are bound; sabre, sword, and knife, are enchanted and bound, in the name of God, the father, the son, and the holy ghost. Amen.

This must be spoken three times.

To Release Spell-bound Persons.

You horseman and footman, whom I here conjured at this time, you may pass on in the name of Jesus Christ, through the word of God and the will of Christ; ride ye on now and pass.

To Compel a Thief to return Stolen Goods.

Early in the morning before sunrise, you must go to a pear tree, and take with you three nails out of a coffin, or three horse-shoe nails that were never used, and holding these towards the rising sun, you must say:

"Oh thief, I bind thee by the first nail, which I drive into thy scull and thy brain, to return the goods thou hast stolen, to their former place; thou shalt feel as sick and as anxious to see men, and to see the place you stole from, as felt the desciple Judas after betraying Jerusalem. I bind thee by the other nail, which I drive into your lungs and liver, to return the stolen goods to their former place; thou shalt feel as sick and as anxious to see men, and to see the place you have stolen from, as did Pilate in the fires of hell. The third nail I shall drive into thy foot, oh thief, in order that thou shalt return the stolen goods to the very same place from which thou hast stolen them. Oh thief, I bind thee, and compel thee, by the three holy nails which were driven through the hands and feet of Jesus Christ, to return the stolen goods to the very same place from which thou hast stolen them." † † † The three nails, however, must be greased with the grease from an excuted criminal or other sinful person.

A Benediction for all purposes.

Jesus, I will arise; Jesus, do thou accompany me; Jesus do thou lock my heart into thine, and let my body and my soul be commended unto thee. The Lord is crucified. May God guard my senses that evil spirits may not overcome me, in the name of God, the father, the son, and the holy ghost. Amen.

To Win every Game one engages in.

Tie the heart of a bat with a red silken string to the right arm, and you will win every game at cards you play.

Against Burns.

Our dear Lord Jesus Christ going on a journey, saw a fire-brand burning: it was Saint Lorenzo stretched out on a roast. He rendered him assistance and consolation; he lifted his divine hand, and blessed the brand; he stopped it from spreading deeper and wider. Thus may the burning be blessed in the name of God, the father, the son, and the holy ghost. Amen.

Another Remedy for Burns.

Clear out brand, but never in; be thou cold or hot, thou must cease to burn. May God guard thy blood and thy flesh, thy marrow and thy bones, and every artery great or small—they all shall be guarded and protected in the name of God, against inflammation and mortification, in the name of God the father, the son, and the holy ghost. Amen.

To be given to Cattle, against Witchcraft.

```
S  A  T  O  R
A  R  E  P  O
T  E  N  E  T
O  P  E  R  A
R  O  T  A  S
```

This must be written on paper and the cattle made to swallow it in their feed.

How to tie up and heal Wounds.

Speak the following: "This wound I tie up in three names, in order that thou mayest take from it, heat, water, falling off of the flesh, swelling, and all that may be injurious about the swelling, in the name of the holy trinity."— This must be spoken three times; then draw a string three times around the wound, and put it under the corner of the house towards the east, and say: "I put thee there, † † † in order that thou mayest take unto thyself the gathered water, the swelling, and the running, and all that may be injurious about the wound. Amen."—Then repeat the Lord's prayer and some good hymnn.

To take the Pain out of a Fresh Wound.

Our dear Lord Jesus Christ had a great many biles and wounds, and yet he never had them dressed. They did not grow old, they were not cut, nor were they ever found running. Jonas was blind, and I spoke to the heavenly child, as true as the five holy wounds were inflicted.

A Benediction against Worms.

Peter and Jesus went out upon the fields; they ploughed three furrows, and ploughed up three worms. The one was white, the other was black, and the third one was red. Now all the worms are dead, in the name † † †. Repeat these words three times.

Against every Evil Influence.

Lord Jesus, thy wounds, so red, will guard me against death.

To retain the Right in Court and Council.

Jesus Nazarenus, Rex Judeorum.

First carry these characters with you, written on paper, and then repeat the following words: "I, (name) appear before the house of the judge. Three dead men look out of the window; one having no tongue, the other having no lungs, and the third was sick, blind and dumb."—This is intended to be used when you are standing before a court in your right, and the judge not being favorably disposed towards you. While on your way to the court, you must repeat the benediction already given above.

To stop Bleeding at any time.

As soon as you cut yourself, you must say: "Blessed wound, blessed hour, blessed be the day on which Jesus Christ was born, in the name † † † Amen.

Another way to Stop blood.

Write the name of the four principle waters of the whole world, flowing out of Paradise, on a paper, namely: Pison, Gihon, Hedekiel, and Pheat, and put it on the wound. In the first book of Moses, the second chapter, verses 11, 12, 13, you will find them. You will find this effective.

Another similar Prescription.

Breathe three times upon the patient, and say the Lord's prayer three times until the words, "upon the earth," and the bleeding will be stoped.

Another still more certain way to stop Bleeding.

If the bleeding will not stop, or if a vein has been cut, then lay the following on it, and it will stop that hour. Yet if any one does not believe this, let him write the letters upon a knife and stab an irrational animal, and he will not be able to draw blood. And whosoever carries this about him, will be safe against all his enemies:

I. m. I. K. I. B. I. P. a. x. v. ss. Ss. vas I. P. O. unay Lit. Dom. mper vobism.

And whenever a woman is going to give birth to a child, or is otherwise afflicted, let her have this letter about her person; it will certainly be of avail.

A peculiar sign to keep back men and animals.

Whenever you are in danger of being attacked, then carry this sign with you: "In the name of God I make the attack. May it please my Redeemer to assist me. Upon the holy assistance of God I depend entirely; upon the holy assistance of God and my gun I rely very truly. God alone be with us. Blessed be Jesus.

Protection of one's House and Hearth.

Beneath thy guardianship, I am safe against all tempests and all enemies, J. J. J.

These three J's signify *Jesus* three times.

A Charm—to be carried about the person.

Carry these words about you, and nothing can hit you: Annania, Azaria, and Misael, blessed be the Lord; for he has redeemed us from hell, and has saved as from death, and he has redeemed us out of the firy furnace, and has preserved us even in the midst of the fire; in the same manner may it please him, the Lord, that there be no fire:

I.

N. I. R.

I.

To Charm Enemies, Robbers and Murderers.

God be with you, brethern; stop, ye thieves, robbers, murderers, horsemen, and soldiers, in all humility, for we have tasted the rosy blood of Jesus. Your rifles and guns will be stopped up with the holy blood of Jesus ; and all swords and arms are made harmless by the five holy wounds of Jesus. There are three roses upon the heart of God: the first is beneficent, the other is omnipotent, and the third is his holy will. You, thieves, must therefore stand under it, standing still as long as I will. In the name of God the father, son, and holy ghost, you are conjured and made to stand.

Protection against all kinds of Weapons.

Jesus, God and man, do thou protect me against all manner of guns, fire arms, long or short, of any kind of metal. Keep thou thine fire, like the Virgin Mary, who kept her fire both before and after her birth. May Christ bind up all fire arms after the manner of his having bound up himself in humility, while in the flesh. Jesus, do thou render harmless all arms and weapons, like unto the husband of Mary the mother of God, he having been harmless likewise. Furthermore, do thou guard the three holy drops of blood which Christ sweated on the Mount of Olives. Jesus Christ! do thou protect me against being killed, and against burning fires. Jesus, do thou not suffer me to be killed, much less to be damned, without having received the Lord's supper. May God the father, son, and holy ghost, assist me in this. Amen.

A Charm against Fire-arms.

Jesus passed over the Red Sea, and looked upon the land and thus must break all ropes and bands, and thus must break all manner of fire-arms, rifles, guns, or pistols, and all false tougues be silenced. May the benediction of God on creating the first man, always be upon me; the benediction spoken by God, when he ordered in a dream that Joseph and Mary together with Jesus should flee into Egypt, be upon me always, and may the holy † be ever lovely and beloved in my right hand. I journey through the country at large where no one is robbed, killed, or murdered,—where no one can do me any injury, and where not even a dog could bite me, or any other animal tear me to pieces. In all things let me be protected, as also my flesh and blood, against sins and false tongues which reach from the earth up to heaven, by the power of the four Evangelists, in the name of God the Father, God the Son, and God the Holy Ghost, Amen.

Another for the same.

I, [name,] conjure ye guns, swords, and knives, as well as all other kinds of arms, by the spear that pierced the side of God, and opened it so that blood and water could flow out, that ye do not injure me, a servant of God, in the † † †. I conjure ye by Saint Stephan, who was stoned by the virgin, that ye cannot injure me who am a servant of God, in the name of † † †. Amen.

A Charm against shooting, cutting or thrusting.

In the name of J. J. J. Amen. I, [name,] Jesus Christ is the true salvation; Jesus Christ governs, reigns, defeats and conquers every enemy, visible or invisible; Jesus, be thou with me at all times, for ever and ever, upon all roads and ways, upon the water and the land, on the mountain and in the valley, in the house and in the yard, in the whole world wherever I am, stand, run, ride or drive; whether I sleep or wake, eat or drink, there be thou also, Lord Jesus Christ, at all times, late and early, every hour, every moment; and in all my goings in or goings out. Those five holy red wounds, oh Lord Jesus Christ, may they guard me against all fire-arms, be they secret or public, that they cannot injure me, or do me any harm whatever, in the name of † † †. May Jesus Christ with his guardianship and protection shield me, (name), always from daily commission of sins, worldly injuries and injustice, from contempt, from pestilence and other diseases, from fear, torture and great suffering, from all evil intentions, from false tongues and old clatter brains; and that no kind of firearms can inflict any injury to my body, do thou take care of me † † †. And that no band of thieves, nor Gipsies, highway robbers, incendiaries, witches and other evil spirits may secretly enter my house or premises, nor break in; may the dear Virgin Mary, and all children who are in heaven with God in eternal joys, protect and guard me against them; and the glory of God the Father shall strengthen me, the wisdom of God the Son shall enlighten me, and the grace of God the Holy Ghost shall empower me from this hour unto all eternity. Amen.

To Charm Guns and other Arms.

The blessing which came from heaven at the birth of Christ, be with me (name). The blessing of God at the creation of the first man, be with ire; the blessing of Christ on being imprisoned, bound, lashed, crowned so dreadfully and beaten, and dieing on the cross, be with me; the blessing which the Priest spoke over the tender, joyful corpse of our Lord Jesus Christ, be with me; the constancy of the holy Mary and all the Saints of God, of the three holy kings, Casper, Melchior, and Balthasar, be with me; the holy four Evangelists, Matthew, Mark, Luke, and John, be with me; the Archangels St. Michael, St. Gabriel, St. Raphael, and St. Uriel, be with me; the twelve holy messengers of the Patriarchs and all the Hosts of Heaven, be with me; and the inexpressible number of all the Saints, be with me. Amen.

Papa, R. tarn, Tetregammaten Angen. Jesus Nazarenus, Rex Judeorum.

To prevent being Cheated, Charmed, or Bewitched, and to be at all times blessed.

Like unto the cup, and the wine, and the holy supper, which our dear Lord Jesus Christ gave unto his dear disciples on Maunday Thursday, may the Lord Jesus guard me in day time and at night, that no dog may bite me, no wild beast tear me to pieces, no tree fall on me, no water rise against me, no fire-arms injure me, no weapons, no steel, no iron cut me, no fire burn me, no false sentence fall upon me, no false tongue injure me, no rogue enrage me, and that no fiends, no witchcraft and enchantment can harm me. Amen.

Different Directions to effect the same.

The Holy Trinity guard me, and be and remain with me on the water and upon the land, in the water or in the fields, in cities or villages, in the whole world wherever I am. The Lord Jesus Christ protect me against all my enemies, secret or public; and may the Eternal Godhead also guard me, through the bitter sufferings of Jesus Christ; his holy rosy blood, shed on the cross, assist me, J. J. Jesus has been crucified, tortured, and died. These are true words; and in the same way must all words be efficacious which are here put down, and spoken in prayer by me. This shall assist me that I shall not be imprisoned, bound, or overcome by any one. Before me all guns and other weapons shall be of no use or power. Fire-arms, hold your fire in the almighty hand of God. Thus all fire-arms shall be charmed. † † †When the right hand of the Lord Jesus Christ was fastened to the tree of the cross; like unto the son of the heavenly father who was obedient unto death, may the eternal Godhead protect me by the rosy blood, by the five holy wounds on the tree of the cross; and thus must I be blessed and well protected, like the cup and the wine, and the genuine true bread, which Jesus Christ gave to his desciples on the evening of Maunday Thursday. J. J. J.

Another Similar Direction.

The grace of God and his benevolence, be with me (N.) I shall now ride or walk out; and I will gird about my loins with a sure ring. So it pleases God, the heavenly father, he will protect me, my flesh and blood, and all my arteries and limbs, during this day and night which I have before me; and however numerous my enemies might be, they must be dumbstruck, and all become like a dead man, white as snow, so that no one will be able to shoot, cut, or throw at me, nor to overcome me, although he may hold rifle or or steel against whosoever else evil weapons and arms might be called, in his hand. My rifle shall go off like the lightning from heaven, and my sword shall cut like a razor. Then went our dear lady Mary upon a very high mountain; she looked down into a very dusky valley, and beheld her dear child standing amidst the Jews, harsh, very harsh, because he was bound so harsh, because he was bound so hard ; and therefore may the dear Lord Jesus Christ save me from all that is injurious to me. † † † Amen.

Another Similar Direction.

There walk out during this day and night, that thou mayest not let any of my enemies, or thieves, approach me, if they do not intend to bring me what was spent from the holy alter. Because God, the Lord Jesus Christ, is ascended into heaven in his living body. O Lord, this is good for me this day and night. † † † Amen.

Another one like it.

In the name of God I walk out. God the father be with me, and God the holy ghost be by my side. Whoever is stronger than these three persons, may approach my body and my life; yet whoso is not stronger than these three, would much better let me be. J. J. J.

A very Safe and reliable Charm.

The peace of our Lord Jesus Christ be with me. [name] Oh shot, stand still! in the name of the mighty prophets Agtion and Elias, and do not kill me! oh shot, stop short! I conjure you by heaven and earth, and by the last judgment, that you do no harm unto me, a child of God. † † †

Another one like it.

I conjure thee, sword, sabre, or knife, that mightest injure or harm me, by the priest of all prayers, who had gone into the temple at Jerusalem, and said: an edged sword shall pierce your soul that you may not injure me, who am a child of God.

A Very Effective Charm.

I, (name,) conjure thee, sword or knife, as well as all other weapons, by that spear which pierced Jesus' side and opened it to the gushing out of blood and water, that he keep me from injury as one of the servants of God. † † † Amen.

A Good Charm against Thieves.

There are three lilies standing upon the grave of the Lord our God: the first one is the courage of God, the other is the blood of God, and the third one is the will of God. Stand still, thief! No more than Jesus Christ stepped down from the cross, no more shalt thou move from this spot:— this I command thee, by the four evangelists and elements of heaven, there in the river, or in the shot, or in the judgment, or in sight. Thus I conjure you by the last judgment to stand still and not to move, until I see all the stars in heaven, and the sun rises again. Thus I stop thy running and jumping, and command it in the name of † † †. Amen.

This must be repeated three times.

How to Recover Stolen Goods.

Take good care to notice through which door the thief passed out, and cut off three small chips from the posts of that door, then take these three chips to a wagon, unbeschrewedly however, take off one of the wheels and put the three chips into the stock of the wheel, in the three highest names, then turn the wheel backwards and say: Thief, thief, thief! Turn back with the stolen goods; thou art forced to do it by the Almighty power of God: † † † God the father calls thee back, God the son turns thee back so that thou must return, and God the holy ghost leads thee back until thou arrive at the place from which thou hast stolen. By the almighty power of God the father thou must come, by the wisdom of God the son thou hast niether peace nor quiet until thou hast returned the stolen goods to their former place, by the grace of God the holy ghost thou must run and jump and canst find no peace or rest until thou arrivest at the place from which thou hast stolen. God the father binds thee, God the son forces thee, and God the holy ghost turns thee back.—(You must not turn the wheel too fast.) Thief, thou must come, † † † thief, thou must come † † † thief, thou must come, † † †. If thou art more almighty, thief, thief, thief, if thou art more almighty than God himself, then you may remain where you are. The ten commandments force thee, thou shalt not steal, and therefore thou must come. † † † Amen.

A well-tried Charm.

Three holy drops of blood have passed down the holy cheeks of the Lord God, and these three holy drops of blood are placed before the touch-hole. As surely as our dear lady was pure from all men, as surely shall no fire or smoke pass out of this barrel. Barrel, do thou give neither fire, nor flame, nor heat. Now I will walk out, because the Lord God goeth before me, God the son is with me, and God the holy ghost is about me forever.

Another well-tried Charm against Fire-Arms.

Blessed is the hour in which Jesus Christ was born; blessed is the hour in which Jesus Christ was born; blessed is the hour in which Jesus Christ has arisen from the dead; blessed are these three hours over thy gun, that no shot or ball shall fly toward me, and neither my skin, nor my hair, nor my blood, nor my flesh, be injured by them, and that no kind of weapon or metal shall do me any harm, so surely as the Mother of God shall not bring forth another son. † † †. Amen.

Charm to gain advantage of a man of superior strength.

I, [name,] breathe upon thee. Three drops of blood I take from thee; the first out of thy heart, the other out of thy liver, and the third out of thy vital powers; and in this I deprive thee of thy strength and manliness.

Hbbi Massa danti Lantien. I. I. I.

A Recipe for destroying Spring-Tails or Ground Fleas.

Take the chaff upon which children have been laying in their cradles, or take the dung of horses, and put that upon the field, and the spring-tails or ground-fleas will no longer do you any injury.

A Benediction for and against all Enemies.

The cross of Christ be with me; the cross of Christ overcomes all water and every fire; the cross of Christ overcomes all weapons; the cross of Christ is a perfect sign and blessing to my soul. May Christ be with me and my body during all my life, at day and at night. Now I pray, I, [name,] pray God the father for the soul's sake, and I pray God the son for the father's sake, and I pray God the holy ghost for the Father's and the Son's sake, that the holy corpse of God may bless me against all evil things, words, and works. The cross of Christ open unto me future bliss ; the cross of Christ banish all evil from me; the cross of Christ be with me, above me, before me, behind me, beneath me, aside of me, and everywhere, and before all my enemies, visible and invisible; these all flee from me as soon as they but know or hear. Enoch and Elias, the two prophets, were never imprisoned, nor bound, nor beaten, and came never out of their power: thus no one of my enemies must be able to injure or attack me in my body or my life, in the name of God the Father, the Son, and the Holy Ghost. Amen.

A Benediction against Enemies, Sickness and Misfortunes.

The blessing which came from heaven, from God the father, when the true living Son was born, be with me at all times; the blessing which God spoke over the whole human race, be with me always. The holy cross of God, as long and as broad, as the one upon which God suffered his blessed, bitter tortures, bless me to-day and forever. The three holy nails which were driven through the holy hands and feet of Jesus Christ, shall bless me to-day and forever. The bitter crown of thorns which was forced upon the holy head of Christ, shall bless me to-day and forever. The spear by which the holy side of Jesus was opened, shall bless me to-day and forever. The rosy blood protect me from all my enemies, and from every thing which might be injurious to my body or soul, or my worldly goods. Bless me, oh ye five holy wounds, in order that all my enemies may be driven away and bound, while God has encompassed all Christendom. In this shall assist me God the Father, the Son, and the Holy Ghost. Amen.—Thus must I, (N.) be blessed as well and as valid as the cup and the wine, and the true, living bread which Jesus gave his desciples on the evening of Maunday Thursday. All those that hate you, must be silent before me; their hearts are dead in regard to me; and their tongues are mute, so that they are not at all able to inflict the least injury upon me, or my house, or my premises: And likewise, all those who intend attacking and wounding me with their arms and weapons, shall be defenceless, weak, and conquered before me. In this shall assist me the holy power of God, which can make all arms or weapons of no avail. All this in the name of God the father, the son, and the holy ghost. Amen.

THE TALISMAN.

It is said that any one going out hunting and carrying it in his game bag, cannot but shoot something worth while, and bring it home.

An old hermit once found an old, lame huntsman in a forest, laying beside the road, and weeping. The hermit asked him the cause of his dejection. Ah me, thou man of God, I am a poor unfortunate being; I must annually furnish my lord with as many deer, and hares, and partridges, as a young and healthy huntsman could hunt up, or else I will be discharged from my office; now I am old and lame, besides game is getting scarce, and I cannot follow it up any longer as I ought to; and I know not what will become of me.—Here the old man's feelings overcome him, and he could not utter another word. The hermit, upon this, took out a small piece of paper, upon which he wrote some words with a pencil, and handing it to the huntsman, he said: there, old friend, put this in your game-bag whenever you go out hunting, and you shall certainly shoot something worth while, and bring it home too; yet be careful to shoot no more than you necessarily need, nor to communicate it to any one that might misuse it, on account of the high meaning contained in these words. The hermit then went on his journey, and after a little the huntsman also arose, and without thinking of any thing particular, he went into the woods, and had scarcely advanced a hundred yards, when he shot as fine a roe-buck as he ever saw in his life. This huntsman was afterwards and during his whole lifetime lucky in his hunting, so much so that he was considered one of the best hunters in that whole country. The following is what the hermit wrote on the paper:

Ut nemo in sense tentat, descendere nemo.

⁎
⁎⁎

† ✝ †

At precedenti spectatur mantica tergo.

The best argument is to try it.

To prevent any one from Killing Game.

Pronounce the name, as for instance Jacob Wohlgemuth, shoot whatever you please; shoot but hair and feathers with and what you give to poor people. † † †Amen.

To Compel a Thief to Return Stolen Goods.

Walk out early in the morning, before sunrise, to a Juniper tree, and bend it with the left hand towards the rising sun, while you are saying: Juniper tree, I shall bend and squeeze thee, until the thief has returned the stolen goods to the place from which he took them.—Then you must take a stone and put it on the bush, and under the bush and the stone you must place the scull of a malefactor. † † † Yet you must be careful in case the thief return the stolen goods, to unloose the bush and replace the stone where it was before.

A Charm against Powder and Ball.

The heavenly and holy trumpet blow every ball and misfortune away from me. I seek refuge beneath the tree of life which bears twelvefold fruits. I stand behind the holy altar of the christian church. I commend myself to the holy trinity. I, [name,] hide myself beneath the holy corpse of Jesus Christ. I commend myself unto the wounds of Jesus Christ, that the hand of no man might be able to sieze me, or to bind me, or to cut me, or to throw me, or to beat me or to overcome me in any way whatever, so help me, [N.]

☞ Whoever carries this book with him, is safe from all his enemies, visible or invisible; and whoever has this book with him, cannot die without the holy corpse of Jesus Christ, nor drownd in any water, nor burn up in any fire, nor can an unjust sentence be passed upon him. So help me.†††

UNLUCKY DAYS,

To be found in each Month.

- January 1 2 3 4 6 11 12.
- February 1 17 18.
- March 14 10.
- April 10 17 18.
- May 7 8.
- June 17.
- July 17 21.
- September 10 18.
- August 20 21.
- October 6.
- November 6 10.
- December 6 11 15.

Whoever is born upon one of these days, is unfortunate and suffers from poverty; and whoever takes sick on one of these days, seldom recovers health; and those who engage or marry on these days, become very poor and miserable. Neither is it advisable to move from one house to another, nor to travel, nor to bargain, nor to engage in a law-suit, on one of these days.

The Signs of the Zodiac must be observed by the course of the moon, as they are daily given in common almanacs.

If a cow calves in the sign of the Virgin, the calf will not live one year; if it happens in the Scorpion, it will die much sooner; therefore no one should be weened off in these signs, nor in the sign of the Capricorn or Aquarius, and they will be in less danger from mortal inflammation.

This is the only piece extracted from a centennial almanac imported from Germany, and there are many who believe in it.

HOHMAN.

In conclusion the following Morning Prayer is given, which is to be spoken before entering upon a Journey. It protects against all manner of bad luck.

Oh Jesus of Nazereth, King of the Jews, yea, a King over the whole world, protect me, (name,) during this day and night, protect me at all times by thy five holy wounds, that I may not be siezed and bound. The holy trinity guard me, that no gun, fire-arm, ball, or lead, shall touch my body; and that they shall be weak like the tears and the bloody sweat of Jesus Christ, in the name of God the father; the son, and the holy ghost. Amen.

APPENDIX.

—◆◆◆—

The following Remedy for Epilepsy was published in the Lancaster, (Pa.) papers, in the year 1828.

TO SUFFERING HUMANITY.

We ourselves know of many unfortunate beings who are afflicted with Epilepsy-yet how many more may be in the country who have perhaps already spent their fortunes in seeking aid in this disease, without gaining relief. We have now been informed of a remedy which is said to be infallible, and which has been adopted by the most distinguished physicians in Europe, and has so well stood the test of repeated trials, that it is now generally applied in Europe. It directs a bedroom for the sick person to be fitted up over the cow stable, where the patient must sleep at night, and should spend the greater part of his time during the day in it. This is easily done by building a regular room over the stable. Then care is to be taken to leave an opening in the ceiling of the stable, in such a manner that the evaporation from the same can pass into the room, while, at the same time, the cow may inhale the perspiration of the sick person. In this way the animal will gradually attract the whole disease, and be affected with arthritic attacks, and when the patient has entirely lost them, the cow will fall dead to the ground. The stable must not be cleaned during the operation, though fresh straw or hay may be put in; and, of course, the milk of the cow, as long as she gives any, must be thrown away as useless.

[Lancaster Eagle.

A Salve to Heal up Wounds.

Take tobacco, green or dry; if green, a good handful; if dry, 2 ounces; together with this take a good handful of elder leaves, fry them well in butter, press it through a cloth, and you may use it as a salve. This will heal up a wound in a short time.

Or go to a white oak tree that stands pretty much isolated, and scrape off the rough bark from the eastern side of the tree, then cut off the thinner bark, break it into small pieces, and boil it until all the strength is drawn out, strain it through a piece of linnen, and boil it again, until it becomes as thick as tar; then take out as much as you need, and put to it an equal proportion of sheep tallow, rosin and wax, and work them together until they form a salve. This salve you put on a piece of linnen, very thinly spread, and lay it on the wound, renewing it occasionally till the wound is healed up.

Or take a handful of parseley, pound it fine, and work it to a salve with an equal proportion of fresh butter. This salve prevents mortification and heals very fast.

PEACHES.

The flowers of the peach tree, prepared like salad, opens the bowels, and is of use in the dropsy. Six or seven pealed kernels of the peach stone, eaten daily, will ease the gravel they are also said to prevent drunkenness, when eaten before meals.

Whoever loses his hair, should pound up peach kernels, mix them: with vinegar, and put them on the bald place. The water distilled from peach flowers, opens the bowels of infants, and destroys their worms.

SWEET OIL.

Sweet oil possesses a great many valuable properties, and it is therefore adviseable for every head of a family to have it at all times about the house, in order that it may be applied in cases of necessity. Here follow some of its chief virtues

It is a sure remedy, internally as well as externally, in all cases of inflammation, in men and animals.

Internally, it is given to allay the burning in the stomach, caused by strong drink or by purging too severely, or by poisonous medicines. Even if pure poison has been swallowed, vomiting may be easily produced by one or two wine glasses of sweet oil, and thus the poison will be carried off, provided it has not already been too long in the bowels; and after the vomiting, a spoonful of the oil should be taken every hour until the burning caused by the poison, is entirely allayed.

Whoever is bit by a snake, or by any other poisonous animal, or by a mad dog, and immediately takes warmed sweet oil, and washes the wound with it, and then puts a rag, three or four times doubled up, and well soaked with oil, on the wound every three or four hours, and drinks a couple of spoonsful of the oil, every four hours, for some days, will surely find out what peculiar virtues the sweet oil possesses in regard to poisons.

In Dysentery, sweet oil is likewise a very useful remedy, when the stomach has first been cleansed by Rheubarb or some other suitable purgative, and then a few spoonsful of sweet oil should be taken every three hours. For this purpose, however, the sweet oil should have been well boiled and a very little hartshorn be mixed with it. This boiled sweet oil is also serviceable in all sorts of bowel complaints and in colics; or when any one receives internal injury as from a fall, a few spoonsful of it should be taken every two hours: for it allays the pain, scatters the coadjulated blood, prevents all inflammation, and heals gently.

Externally, it is applicable in all manner of swellings; it softens, allays the pain, and prevents inflammation.

Sweet oil and white lead ground together, makes a very good salve, which is applicable in burns or scalds. This salve is also excellent against infection from poisonous weeds or waters, if it is put on the infected part as soon as it is noticed.

If sweet oil is put in a large glass, so as to fill it about one half full, and the glass is then filled up with the flowers of the St. Johnswort, and well covered and placed in the sun for about four weeks, the oil proves then, when distilled, such a valuable remedy for all fresh wounds in men and animals, that no one can imagine its medicinal powers who has not tried it. This should at all times be found in a well conducted household. In a similar manner, an oil may be made of white lilies, which is likewise very useful to soften hardened swellings and burns, and to cure the sore breasts of women.

CURE FOR DROPSY.

Dropsy is a disease derived from a cold humidity, which passes through the different limbs to such a degree that it either swells the whole or a portion of them. The usual symptoms and precursers of every case of dropsy, are the swelling of the feet and thighs, and then of the face; besides this the change of the natural colour of the flesh into a dull white, with great thirst, loss of appetite, costiveness, sweating, throwing up of slimy substances, but little urine, laziness and aversion to exercise.

Physicians know three different kinds of dropsy, which they name:

> I. *Anasarca,* when the water penetrates between the skin and the flesh over the whole body, and all the limbs, and even about the face, and swells them.

2. *Ascites*, when the belly and thighs swell, while the upper extremities dry up.
3. *Tympanites*, caused rather by wind than water. The belly swells up very hard, the navel is forced out very far, and the other members fall away. The belly becomes so much inflated, that knocking against it causes a sound like that of a large drum, and from this circumstance its name is derived.

The chief thing in curing dropsy, rests upon three points, namely:

1. To reduce the hardness of the swelling which may be in the bowels or other parts.
2. To endeavor to scatter the humours.
3. To endeavor to pass them off either through the stool or through the urine.

The best cure therefore must chiefly consist in this: To avoid as much as possible all drinking, and use only dry vituals; to take moderate exercise, and to sweat and purge the body considerably.

If any one feels symptoms of dropsy, or while it is yet in its first stages, let him make free use of the sugar of the herb called *Fumatory*, as this purifies the blood; and the *Euphrasy* sugar to open the bowels.

A CURE FOR DROPSY. — *(Said to be Infallible.)*

Take a jug of stone or earthen ware, and put four quarts of strong healthy cider into it; take two handsful of parsely roots and tops, cut it fine; a handful of scraped horse-raddish, two table-spoonsful of bruised mustard seed, half an ounce of squills, and half an ounce of juniper berries put all these in the jug, and place it near the fire for 24 hours, so as to keep the cider warm, and shake it up often; then strain it through a cloth and keep it for use.

To a grown person give half a wine glass full three times a day, on an empty stomach. But if necessary you may increase the dose, although it must decrease again as soon as the water is carried off; and, as stated before, use dry vituals and exercise gently.

This remedy has cured a great many persons, and among others a woman of 70 years of age, who had the dropsy so badly, that she was afraid to get out of bed, for fear her skin might burst, and whom it was thought could not live but a few days. She used this remedy according to the directions given, and in less than a week the water had passed off her, the swelling of her stomach fell, and in a few weeks afterwards she again enjoyed perfect health.

Or: Drink for a few days very strong Bohea tea, and eat the leaves of it. This simple means is said to have carried away the water from some persons in three or four days, and freed them from the swelling, although the disease had reached the highest pitch.

Or: Take three spoonsful of rape seed, and half an ounce of clean gum myrrh, put these together in a quart of good old wine, and let it stand over night in the room, keeping it well covered. Aged persons are to take 2 spoonsful of this an hour after supper, and the same before going to bed; younger persons must diminish the quantity according to their age, and continue the use of it as long as necessary.

Or: Take young branches of spruce pine, cut them into small pieces, pour water on them and let them boil a while, then pour it into a large tub, take off your clothes, and sit down over it, covering yourself and the tub with a sheet or blanket, to prevent the vapour from escaping. When the water begins to cool, let some one put in hot bricks; and when you have thus been sweating for a while, wrap the sheet or blanket close around you and go to bed with it. A repetition of this for several days will free the system from all water.

The following Valuable Recipes, not in the original work of Hohman, are added by the publishers.

CURE FOR DROPSY.

Take of the broom-corn seed, well powdered and sifted, one drachm. Let it steep twelve hours in a wine glass and a half of good rich wine, and take it in the morning fasting, having first shaken it so that the whole may be swallowed. Let the patient walk after it, if able, or let him use what exercise he can without fatigue, for an hour and a half; after which let him take 2 oz. of olive oil; and not eat or drink any thing in less that half an hour afterwards. Let this be repeated every day, or once in three days, and not oftener, till a cure is effected; and do not let blood, or use any other remedy during the course.

Nothing can be more gentle and safe than the operation of this remedy. If the dropsy is in the body, it discharges it by urine, without any inconvenience: if it is between the skin and flesh, it causes blisters to rise on the legs, by which it will run off; but this does not happen to more than one in thirty: and in this case no plasters must be used, but apply red cabbage leaves. It cures dropsy in pregnant women, without injury to the mother or child. It also alleviates asthma, consumption, and disorders of the liver.

REMEDY FOR THE LOCK JAW.

We are informed by a friend that a sure preventive against this terrible disease, is, to take some soft soap, and mix it with a sufficient quantity of pulverized chalk, so as to make it of the consistency of buckwheat batter; keep the chalk moistened with a fresh supply of soap until the wound begins to discharge, and the patient finds relief. Our friend stated to us that explicit confidence may be placed in what he says, that he has known several cases where this remedy has been successfully applied. So simple and so valuable a remedy, within the reach of every person, ought to be generally known.

[N. Y. Evening Post.

FOR THE STING OF A WASP OR BEE.

A Liverpool paper states as follows:—"A few days ago happening to be in the country, we witnessed the efficacy of the remedy for the sting of a wasp mentioned in one of our late papers. A little boy was stung severely and was in great torture, until an onion was applied to the part affected, when the cure was instantaneous. This important and simple remedy cannot be too generally known, and we pledge ourselves to the fact above stated."

You have now read The Long Lost Friend *as Johann*
Georg Hohman first intended:
clear, simple, earnest, and rooted in the daily faith of his
people.
The facsimile preserved the past; the modern typeset made
the old words plain.
Now you stand at the threshold of something new.

The tradition Hohman carried did not end with him.
It lived in whispered prayers over children's beds,
in psalms spoken by lamplight,
in blessings murmured before the start of a workday,
and in quiet acts of devotion passed from parent to child.
It lived because ordinary people kept using it—
not as relic or superstition,
but as a way of drawing near to God in the worries and
needs of everyday life.

The world of 2025 is not the world of 1820,
yet the human heart remains the same.
We still seek peace.
We still long for protection.
We still need strength for our labors
and comfort for our fears.
Hohman addressed the dangers of his time;
we address the dangers of ours.

This expansion does not rewrite his tradition;
it continues it.
Everything that follows is drawn from the same well—
from scripture,
from long-standing Christian practice,
and from the steady, Christ-centered Braucherei that shaped
Hohman's world.
No foreign rituals have been added.
No borrowed ceremonies have been inserted.
Only the living essence of the original remains,
applied to the needs of the present age.

As you move from the old text into the renewal that follows,
may your heart remain open,
your spirit at peace,
and your mind attentive to the gentle workings of God
in the ordinary moments of life.

Proceed now with readiness of heart—
and may the blessings of the Lord accompany you
into the pages ahead.

Using This Book in Daily Life

This book was never meant to sit untouched on a shelf. It was written to be **held**, **spoken aloud**, **shared**, and **woven into daily life**. The people who first used it did so with simple faith, steady hands, and open hearts. You may do the same.

Here are gentle ways to approach this text devotionally:

Read Slowly and With Peace

Choose one charm, prayer, or psalm at a time.
Let the words settle in your mind and spirit.
You do not need to rush; blessings are not hurried things.

Speak the Words Aloud

Braucherei is a spoken tradition.
A prayer whispered becomes a prayer lived.
Let the sound of the words steady your breathing and quiet your thoughts.

Use Simple Gestures

A hand on the heart.
A hand on the brow.
A small cross traced in the air.
These gestures are reminders—not magic tricks—calling the mind back to
God's presence.

Let Scripture Be the Foundation

Every charm and blessing in this book stands upon scripture.
If a passage speaks to you, return to it often.
Write it down.
Carry it.
Pray it.

Keep Your Heart Free From Harmful Intent

This tradition is rooted in peace, not control;
in comfort, not manipulation.
Use everything in these pages
with gentleness,
humility, and
sincerity.

Bless Your Home and Your Loved Ones

You may speak these prayers over:

- your home,
- your work,
- your family,
- your rest,
- your peace,
- your worries.

Think of this book not as a tool, but as a companion—a guide that stands beside you in the ordinary places of life.

Remember That God Meets You Where You Are

Whether you use these words in a moment of fear, grief, anxiety, or hope, let them be openings through which God's presence may enter.

This book does not demand expertise.
It simply invites your sincerity.

SECTION I
PRAYERS OF PROTECTION
FOR THE HOUSEHOLD

A Prayer to Guard the Home from All Harm

(For the front door, spoken morning or evening)

Place the right hand upon the doorframe
and say with faith:

"As the LORD watched over Israel by night and by day,
so let His watch be upon this house.
Let no mischief enter here,
neither through word nor thought,
neither through foot nor hand.
Let peace be established as the cornerstone,
and truth as the beam above."

Then recite **Psalm 121** aloud,
and conclude:

"Christ be my shield, Christ be my wall,
Christ be the fire at the gate,
and the calm within the rooms."

Make the sign of the cross over the entrance,
or trace an unseen cross in the air,
and say:

"So shall it stand in the name of the Father,
and of the Son,
and of the Holy Ghost. Amen."

A Protection Against Accidents
in Driving and Travel

Before traveling, place your hand on the steering wheel:

"As the LORD guided the paths of His servants
through wilderness and storm,
let Him guide this journey also.
Let the angels that kept Paul in shipwreck
keep me upon the road.
Let the eyes of the wicked not see me,
nor the hand of the careless strike me.
May this vehicle be as a chariot of peace,
and may the way open before me."

Then speak the words of **Psalm 91** (abridged):

"He shall give His angels charge over thee,
to keep thee in all thy ways."

Finish with:

"In the name of Jesus,
I shall come home in safety,
for the Lord is my guard."

Blessing for Children at School
(or Away From Home)

(For daily departure, laying on of hands included)

Place your hand lightly on the child's shoulder or head.

Say:

"The peace of Christ go with you,
the wisdom of Christ teach you,
and the strength of Christ keep you.
Let no confusion come near your mind,
nor any unkind word cling to your heart.
May your steps be steady,
and your spirit brave.
May the Lord send His angel
to walk beside you
as He did with young Tobias on his journey."

Then recite:

"The LORD bless thee and keep thee;
the LORD make His face shine upon thee
and give thee peace." *(Numbers 6:24-26)*

Seal it with:

"Go in grace. Return in gladness."

A Charm Against Slander and Evil Speech

(Including digital gossip, false accusation, and harmful tongues)

Stand facing east in the morning light, or toward a window if indoors.

Say:

"Hide me, O LORD, from the strife of tongues.
Let no false word take root,
nor any angry speech find strength against me.
Turn aside the arrow of gossip,
the whisper of the jealous,
and the message sent in secret.
Let truth stand as a wall before me,
and justice as my rear guard."
(Psalm 31:20; Isaiah 52:12)

Then speak:

"The tongue is a small fire,
but the Spirit quenches all flames of harm."
(James 3:5)

Finish with:

"I bind the power of wicked speech,
both spoken and written,
both posted and shared,
and I loose the peace of Christ over my name.
In His light, I am kept."

Safeguard of the Home Network and Devices

Place your hand upon the modem, router, or the central device through which most communication passes.

Say:

"Lift up your heads, O gates;
be lifted up, O doors,
that the King of Glory may come in."
(Psalm 24:7)

Then:

"Let no confusion, no malice,
no deceitful message,
nor any harmful image
enter through this gate.
Let this connection serve peace and wisdom,
and not fear.
Let every device in this house
be a servant of good and not of trouble."

Trace a small cross in the air over the device and pray:

"The LORD bless thee and keep thee.
His peace guard every path of word and picture.
In Christ's name. Amen."

Prayer for Peace Between Neighbors

*(For tension, misunderstanding,
arguments, or boundary disputes)*

Stand at the threshold of your home or within earshot of the dispute's
direction.

Say:

"Blessed are the peacemakers,
for they shall be called the children of God."
(Matthew 5:9)

Then speak with calm authority:

"Let every harsh word soften,
and every anger be stilled.
Let understanding rise as morning light,
and let grudges fall away like shadows.
Where there is offense, let there be pardon.
Where there is confusion, let there be clarity.
Where there is bitterness, let there be mercy."

Raise your right hand gently and say:

"As much as lieth in me,
I seek peace with all.
May the Lord who quieted the storm
quiet this ground,
and give peace within these borders."

(Romans 12:18; Psalm 147:14)

Keeping the Workplace Free from Malice

(For jobs involving customers,
co-workers, managers, or constant pressure)

Before beginning the day's labor, place your hand upon the tools of your trade (computer, uniform, keys, clipboard, workstation, etc.).

Say:

"Let the favor of the LORD our God be upon us,
and establish the work of our hands."
(Psalm 90:17)

Then:

"Let no envy rise against me,
nor any hidden scheme find success.
Let the spirit of strife be turned away,
and let peace rest upon this place.
Make my speech gentle,
my judgment wise,
and my heart steady.
Let every task be done as unto the Lord,
and may His protection cover my labor."
(Colossians 3:23)

Finish by touching your chest and saying:

"Christ before me,
Christ behind me,
Christ at my side in the day's work.
Amen."

SECTION II
CHARMS OF HEALING
AND COMFORT

For Anxiety and Sudden Fear

Place your right hand over your heart and breathe slowly.

Say:

"I sought the LORD, and He heard me,
and delivered me from all my fears."
(Psalm 34:4)

"What time I am afraid,
I will trust in Thee."
(Psalm 56:3)

Then lay your left hand gently over your right hand and speak:

"Let this fear be loosed from me,
and let the peace of Christ settle upon my mind.
No terror of thought,
nor shadow of imagination,
shall rule over me.
I breathe in His light,
and breathe out all fright.
In His name, I am steadied."

For Sleeplessness and Troubled Mind

Sit at the bedside or lie down in stillness.

Say:

"I will both lay me down in peace, and sleep:
for Thou, LORD, only makest me dwell in safety."
(Psalm 4:8)

Then trace a small cross over your forehead with your finger and say:

"Let the night bring rest,
not fear.
Let my thoughts be quieted,
and my heart be calmed.
Let no terror of darkness disturb me,
nor any dream trouble my sleep.
In Christ's keeping I lay myself,
and in Christ's keeping I rise."

For Depression and Heaviness of Spirit

Stand upright, hands open at your sides.

Say:

"Why art thou cast down, O my soul?
Hope thou in God,
for I shall yet praise Him."
(Psalm 42:11)

Lift your hands slowly upward and speak:

"Give unto me, O LORD,
the oil of joy for mourning,
the garment of praise
for the spirit of heaviness."
(Isaiah 61:3)

Then place your hands gently upon your chest:

"Let this heaviness be lifted,
and let Your light return to me.
Restore my strength.
Renew my breath.
Bring back the joy of Your salvation."

For Addiction and Temptation

Place your hand upon your own brow,
or upon the hand of one who seeks help.

Say:

"No temptation hath taken you
but such as is common to man:
but God is faithful,
who will not suffer you to be tempted above what you are able."
(1 Corinthians 10:13)

Then speak firmly:

"Sin shall not have dominion over you."
(Romans 6:14)

Lay your hand upon your own chest and say:

"In the name of Jesus,
I bind the craving,
I bind the urge,
I bind every chain that would enslave the heart.
And I loose freedom,
clean desire,
and the strength to walk in newness of life.
Amen."

For Pain in the Bones or Nerves

Place your right hand directly upon the place of pain.

Say:

"Jesus said, I will; be thou clean."
(Mark 1:41)

Then:

**"In the name of Christ,
rise up and be strengthened."**
(Acts 3:6)

Move your hand in a slow outward motion away from the pain,
as though sweeping it aside, and speak:

**"Let all sharpness depart.
Let all burning depart.
Let all stiffness depart.
Peace to this flesh,
comfort to these bones,
ease to these nerves,
in the name of the Healer."**

For Healing of Broken Relationships

Stand or sit in quietness, holding your hands open.

Say:

"Be kind one to another,
tenderhearted,
forgiving one another,
even as God for Christ's sake
hath forgiven you."
(Ephesians 4:32)

Then:

"Let bitterness be dissolved,
and let peace be restored.
Heal the wound between us,
mend the torn places,
and give grace for honest speech.
Let what was broken be made whole,
and let mercy triumph over judgment."

If appropriate, speak aloud the names of those involved.

Finish with:

"In Christ's light we walk toward peace."

For a Child's Health and Calmness

Place your hand gently upon the child's head or back.

Say:

"The LORD is your shepherd;
you shall not want.
He makes you to lie down in safety,
and He restores your soul."
(Psalm 23)

Then speak softly:

"May the Lord who took children in His arms
take you now in His peace."
(Mark 10:16)

Stroke the child's back or arm three times, slowly, and say:

"Peace be to your mind,
peace be to your breath,
peace be to your body.
The Lord watches over you,
and His angels surround you."

SECTION III
CHARMS OF GOOD FORTUNE
AND LIVELIHOOD

For Finding Steady Work and Daily Bread

Place your hand upon the tools of your trade
or upon your chest if unemployed.

Say:

"Let the favor of the LORD our God be upon us,
and establish Thou the work of our hands."
(Psalm 90:17)

Then speak:

"Give us this day our daily bread."
(Matthew 6:11)

Lift your right hand and say:

"Open a door no man can shut.
Make a way where none appears.
Lead me to honest labor,
and bless the work set before me.
Let peace be in my heart,
strength in my hands,
and provision in my house."

For Success in Legal Matters

Before entering any place of judgment,
place your right hand over your heart.

Say:

"Plead my cause, O LORD, with them that strive with me."
(Psalm 35:1)

Then:

"The king's heart is in the hand of the LORD:
He turneth it whithersoever He will."
(Proverbs 21:1)

Take one steady breath and speak:

"Give me calm speech,
clear mind,
and steady spirit.
Let truth stand beside me,
and peace go before me.
Turn hearts toward fairness,
and judgment toward mercy."

For Honest Trade and Fair Contracts

Place your hand upon the contract, ledger, or place of transaction.

Say:

"Ye shall do no unrighteousness in judgment,
in measure or in weight."
(Leviticus 19:35)

Then:

"Whatsoever ye do,
do it heartily, as unto the Lord."
(Colossians 3:23)

Trace a small cross over the document or space and say:

"Let this agreement be clean,
without deceit.
Let both parties walk in honesty,
and may the Lord prosper dealings done in righteousness.
Let greed be cast out,
and truth be established."

To Protect Money and Prevent Theft of Identity

Hold your wallet, purse, or phone in your hand.

Say:

"The LORD shall preserve thee from all evil:
He shall preserve thy going out and thy coming in."
(Psalm 121:7–8)

Then:

"He keepeth the paths of judgment
and preserveth the way of His saints."
(Proverbs 2:8)

Touch your hand to your chest and say:

"Let no deceitful hand reach what is mine,
nor any false name or number be taken.
Let what I earn be kept,
and what I guard be protected.
In righteousness I walk,
and in peace I am kept."

A Prayer for Blessing of Tools and Instruments

(Cars, phones, laptops, musical gear, work equipment)

Place your hand upon the tool or device.

Say:

"The LORD shall bless all the work of thy hand."
(Deuteronomy 28:12)

Then:

**"Let this tool be a servant of good,
not of trouble.
Let it work smoothly,
and carry no confusion.
Let it be used with wisdom,
and kept in peace.
The Lord is my shepherd:
I shall not want."**
(Psalm 23:1)

Make the sign of the cross over the tool or trace it in the air.

For Lost or Misplaced Things

Stand still, breathe once, and say:

"Nothing is hidden from the eye of God,
nor lost from His memory."

Then call softly:

"By the mercy of Christ,
let that which is missing
return to my hand."

Walk through the house or place where it may be, repeating:

"What was lost shall be found,
and what is hidden shall come forth."

If the object belongs to another, speak their name aloud.

A Charm Before Speaking to Officials or Employers

Place your hand lightly upon your mouth.

Say:

"I will be with thy mouth,
and teach thee what thou shalt say."
(Exodus 4:12)

Then:

"The Holy Ghost shall teach you
in the same hour what ye ought to say."
(Luke 12:12)

Remove your hand and speak:

"Let my words be seasoned with grace,
my mind be steady,
and my heart be calm.
Let fear depart,
and clarity remain.
The Lord is my helper:
I shall not be ashamed."

SECTION IV
CHARMS FOR TECHNOLOGY AND THE MODERN LIFE

Blessing of the Phone (Gate of Words)

Hold the phone in your hand and breathe once in peace.

Say:

"Let the words of my mouth
and the meditation of my heart
be acceptable in Thy sight,
O LORD, my strength and my redeemer."
(Psalm 19:14)

Lay your hand over the phone and say:

"Let this device carry peace,
not anger.
Let messages be gentle,
not cruel.
Let the words that enter or leave this gate
bring wisdom and truth.
Let no bitterness be spoken here,
and no harm be stirred.
As a soft answer turns away wrath,
so let this phone be an instrument of calm."
(Proverbs 15:1)

Blessing of the Laptop (Gate of Works)

Place your hand upon the keyboard.

Say:

"Let the beauty of the LORD our God be upon us,
and establish Thou the work of our hands."
(Psalm 90:17)

Then:

"Whatever I do,
I do it heartily, as unto the Lord."
(Colossians 3:23)

Trace a small cross over the screen and speak:

"Let this work be done in clarity,
not confusion.
Let the labor be fruitful,
not hindered.
Let my mind be steady,
and my hands guided.
Let this tool serve good,
and do no harm."

Blessing of the Router (Gate of Connection)

Place your right hand upon the router, modem, or central connection point.

Say:

"Lift up your heads, O gates;
and be lifted up,
that the King of Glory may come in."
(Psalm 24:7)

Then speak:

"Let this gate be guarded.
Let every connection be clean.
Let no deceitful thing enter here,
nor any harmful intent pass through.
Let the peace of Christ reign in this house,
from the first signal to the last."

For Protection Against Cyber-Harassment

Stand facing your screen or hold your phone in your hand.

Say:

"Thou shalt hide me in the secret of Thy presence
from the strife of tongues."
(Psalm 31:20)

Then:

"Let the arrows of bitter words
fall harmlessly to the ground.
Let every malicious message fail,
and every wicked intention be undone.
Let truth be my shield,
and peace be my guard.
No power of the tongue,
nor written word,
nor hidden post
shall prosper against me."

Finish with:

"In Christ's peace I stand."

For Peace on Social Media

Hold the phone or device in your hand.

Say:

"Blessed are the peacemakers,
for they shall be called the children of God."
(Matthew 5:9)

Then speak:

"Let my words be gentle,
and my heart slow to anger.
Let no confusion rise within me,
nor any wrath be stirred by what I see.
As much as lieth in me,
let me live peaceably with all."
(Romans 12:18)

Touch the screen lightly and say:

"Let peace guide what I post
and what I receive."

For Freedom From the Fear of Missing Out

Sit quietly with the device set aside.

Say:

**"The LORD is my shepherd;
I shall not want."**
(Psalm 23:1)

Then:

**"Seek ye first the kingdom of God,
and His righteousness;
and all these things shall be added unto you."**
(Matthew 6:33)

Place your hand upon your chest:

**"Let comparison depart,
let envy fall away,
and let my heart find rest.
What is mine will come,
and what is not mine will pass.
In peace I stand,
and in peace I am kept."**

To Keep the Mind Clear
From Excessive Screens

Turn off the device or place it face-down.

Say:

"Be still, and know that I am God."
(Psalm 46:10)

Then:

"Let my mind dwell on what is true,
honest,
just,
pure,
lovely,
and of good report."
(Philippians 4:8)

Touch your brow and speak:

"Let the noise depart,
and the clamor cease.
Let my mind be cleared,
and my thoughts renewed.
The Lord is my stillness,
and my clarity."

SECTION V
CLEANSING & DELIVERANCE

A Charm for Cleansing the House From Strife

Stand in the center of the house or at the place where discord lingers.

Say:

"Behold, how good and how pleasant it is
for brethren to dwell together in unity."
(Psalm 133:1)

Walk slowly from room to room (or trace a cross in the air) and speak:

"Let every harsh word fall away.
Let anger be stilled.
Let peace return to these walls.
Let the Lord make this dwelling
a quiet habitation,
a place of sure rest."
(Isaiah 32:18)

Finish at the doorway, saying:

"Peace be to this house,
and to all who dwell within."

For Driving Away Dark Thoughts and Despair

Sit in a quiet place and put your hand upon your heart.

Say:

**"The LORD is my light and my salvation;
whom shall I fear?"**
(Psalm 27:1)

Then:

**"Come unto Me, all ye that labor
and are heavy laden,
and I will give you rest."**
(Matthew 11:28)

Breathe gently and speak:

**"Let every dark thought depart.
Let every shadow flee.
Let the peace of Christ rise within me
as the dawn rises over night.
I am not forsaken.
I am not alone.
In His light, I stand."**

To Quiet a Tormented Mind

Lay your right hand upon your brow.

Say:

"God is our refuge and strength,
a very present help in trouble."
(Psalm 46:1)

Then:

"Let the peace of God,
which passeth all understanding,
keep my heart and mind
through Christ Jesus."
(Philippians 4:7)

Close your eyes and speak softly:

"Let the racing cease,
let the clamor fall,
let quietness return to me.
In Christ, my mind is steadied.
In Christ, my breath is calm."

Deliverance From Obsession or Spiritual Oppression

Stand upright with feet firm, or sit with your back straight.

Say with authority:

"The Lord rebuke thee."
(Mark 1:25)

Then place your hand upon your chest:

**"Behold, He has given me power
to tread on serpents and scorpions,
and over all the power of the enemy."**
(Luke 10:19)

Speak firmly:

**"In the name of Jesus Christ,
let every unclean thought,
every troubling presence,
every binding fear,
depart from me now.
No darkness has claim on me.
No spirit of torment may stand.
I am kept by the power of God.
Amen."**

Cleansing Objects Brought Into the Home

Sources: Acts 19:11-12; 1 Samuel 7:3; Christian consecration practices.

Hold the object in your hand or before you.

Say:

"Prepare your hearts unto the LORD,
and put away strange things."
(1 Samuel 7:3)

Then:

"Let all harm be removed from this object.
Let every troubling influence be cast out.
Let it be cleansed by the mercy of God
and kept in His peace."

Touch the object lightly and speak:

"As handkerchiefs brought healing
in the days of the apostles,
so let this object bear no burden,
but only peace."
(Acts 19:11-12)

Prayer After a Quarrel

Stand facing the doorway or sit in stillness.

Say:

"Be angry, and sin not:
let not the sun go down upon your wrath."
(Ephesians 4:26)

Then speak:

"Let mercy and truth meet,
and righteousness and peace kiss each other."
(Psalm 85:10)

Place your hand upon your heart:

"Let the heat depart from me.
Let the hurt lessen.
Let my spirit be gentle
and my judgment wise.
Restore peace within me,
and set right what has gone astray."

For Peace of the Departed and Comfort of the Living

Hold a picture, candle, or simply stand in quiet remembrance.

Say:

**"The LORD is my shepherd;
I shall not want."**

Then speak:

**"Peace I leave with you,
My peace I give unto you."**
(John 14:27)

Lift your hand slightly and say:

**"May the departed rest in Your light,
and may the living be comforted.
Let sorrow be eased,
let grief be gentled,
let memory be blessed
and not burdensome.
In Christ we live,
and to Christ we return."**

SECTION VI
SCRIPTURAL TALISMANS

The Five Psalms of Protection

*(Psalms long used in Christian folk-magic
for shielding and deliverance)*

Read any of these aloud when protection is needed,
or carry them written upon clean paper.

Psalm 3 — Against Fear and Rising Trouble

"Thou, O LORD, art a shield for me;
my glory, and the lifter up of mine head."
(Psalm 3:3)

Psalm 27 — For Courage and Light

"The LORD is my light and my salvation;
whom shall I fear?"
(Psalm 27:1)

Psalm 91 — For Angelic Guard and Deliverance

"He shall give His angels charge over thee,
to keep thee in all thy ways."
(Psalm 91:11)

Psalm 121 — For Journey and Daily Safety

"The LORD shall preserve thy going out
and thy coming in."
(Psalm 121:8)

Psalm 140 — For Deliverance From Malice

"Deliver me, O LORD,
from the evil man:
preserve me from the violent man."
(Psalm 140:1)

Keep one psalm near the door or speak it before travel.

The Seven Psalms of Healing

(Used for illness of body, mind, or spirit)

Read one psalm each day, or all seven when healing is urgently sought.

Psalm 6 — For Mercy and Relief

"Heal me, O LORD;
for my bones are vexed."

Psalm 30 — For Restoration and Strength

"O LORD my God, I cried unto Thee,
and Thou hast healed me."

Psalm 41 — For Sickness and Weakness

"The LORD will strengthen him
upon the bed of languishing."

Psalm 103 — For Renewal and Blessing

"Who healeth all thy diseases."

Psalm 107 — For Deliverance From Affliction

"He sent His word, and healed them."

Psalm 147 — For Brokenness and Wounds

"He healeth the broken in heart,
and bindeth up their wounds."

Psalm 23 — For Peace in Body and Spirit

"He restoreth my soul."

May these be spoken over the sick, written and carried, or read in quiet prayer.

The Words of Jesus for Peace **and Anxiety**

(For fear, turmoil, doubt, or the need for reassurance)

Speak slowly, with steady breath.

"Let not your heart be troubled."

(John 14:1)

"Peace I leave with you, My peace I give unto you."

(John 14:27)

"Lo, I am with you alway, even unto the end of the world."

(Matthew 28:20)

"Come unto Me, all ye that labor and are heavy laden, and I will give you rest."

(Matthew 11:28)

"Be not afraid; only believe."

(Mark 5:36)

Let these be spoken whenever fear rises within,
or repeated until calm returns.

Paul's Armor of God as a Shielding Charm

(Long used as spoken protection in Christian tradition)

Stand upright and speak with resolve:

**"Be strong in the Lord,

and in the power of His might."**

Place your hand upon your heart:

"I put on the breastplate of righteousness."

Touch your forehead:

"I take the helmet of salvation."

Touch both hands:

**"I hold the shield of faith,
wherewith I quench all the fiery darts of the wicked."**

Lift your hand as though grasping light:

**"I take the sword of the Spirit,
which is the word of God."**

Pray:

**"And having done all,
I stand."**

This may be spoken at the start of each day for protection.

The Priest's Blessing (Numbers 6:24–26)

(A universal Christian benediction for safety, peace, and divine favor)

Raise your right hand or trace a cross in the air.

Say:

"The LORD bless thee and keep thee;
the LORD make His face shine upon thee
and be gracious unto thee;
the LORD lift up His countenance upon thee
and give thee peace."

This may be spoken over oneself, one's family, one's home, or anyone seeking blessing.

SECTION VII
TRADITIONAL BRAUCHEREI
PRACTICES RENEWED

Laying-on-of-Hands Technique

Place your right hand gently upon the place of need, or upon the shoulder
if for general blessing.

Say:

"They shall lay hands on the sick,
and they shall recover."
(Mark 16:18)

Then breathe once, slowly, and speak:

"Peace to this flesh.
Peace to this mind.
Peace to this heart.
In the name of Jesus Christ,
be strengthened."

This may be used for comfort, healing, courage, or calm.

The Threefold Breath Prayer

Stand or sit quietly and inhale through the nose.

With each breath, say:

First Breath

"Lord, give me peace."

Second Breath

"Lord, give me strength."

Third Breath

"Lord, give me light."

Then speak:

"As You breathed life into Adam,
and breathed peace upon Your disciples,
breathe upon me now."
(Genesis 2:7; John 20:22)

Use whenever the spirit feels troubled, weary, or clouded.

The Water Charm for Purity

Hold a cup or small bowl of clean water.

Say:

"Purge me with hyssop,
and I shall be clean."
(Psalm 51:7)

Then:

"Whosoever drinketh of the water
that I shall give him
shall never thirst."
(John 4:14)

Dip your fingers lightly in the water and touch your forehead, saying:

"Let all clouded thought be cleared,
let all heaviness be lifted,
let all trouble be washed away."

Dispose of the water respectfully after use.

The Salt Line of Protection

Hold salt in your hand.

Say:

"The LORD hath healed these waters."
(2 Kings 2:21)

Then cast a thin line of salt across the threshold or perimeter as needed,
saying:

**"Let no harm pass this line.
Let no malice cross this boundary.
As salt preserves from corruption,
so let this house be kept."**
(Matthew 5:13)

Sweep away after the danger or conflict has passed.

The Egg Charm for Removing Heavy Spirit

Hold a fresh egg in your hand.

Speak:

"The Lord is my light and my salvation."
(Psalm 27:1)

Pass the egg slowly over the head, chest, and back, without touching the skin, saying:

**"Let heaviness depart.
Let sorrow loosen.
Let trouble withdraw from flesh and mind.
In Christ's name,
let this burden be lifted."**

Dispose of the egg by cracking it into running water or burying it in earth away from the home.

The Psalmic Circle of the Home

Walk clockwise through the home or property line.

At each corner or turning, say:

"As the mountains are round about Jerusalem,
so the LORD is round about His people."
(Psalm 125:2)

Then:

"The angel of the LORD encampeth
round about them that fear Him."
(Psalm 34:7)

Upon completing the circle, stand at the front entrance and say:

"Lord, be the guard of this dwelling,
the peace of its rooms,
and the keeper of all who enter."

The Blessing of Tools, Vehicles, and Daily Labor

Place your hand upon the tool, vehicle, or object used in daily work.

Say:

"The LORD shall bless all the work of thy hand."
(Deuteronomy 28:12)

Then:

**"He leadeth me beside still waters;
He restoreth my soul."**
(Psalm 23)

Touch the object lightly and speak:

**"Let this work be done in peace,
with strength,
with clarity,
and with good success.
Let this tool serve righteousness,
and do no harm.
In Christ's name. Amen."**

THE SEVEN ANGELIC DAYS
A Christian Germanic Devotional Cycle

For centuries, Christians across Europe—especially in the German-speaking world—kept weekly devotional rhythms shaped not only by scripture and the liturgical calendar but also by the ministry of the archangels. These correspondences were not occult, secret, or esoteric; they appeared openly in prayer books, rosaries, hymnals, and household devotions. Families prayed through the week with a sense that God assigned His holy angels to guide, protect, and comfort His people in the ordinary concerns of life.

What follows is a gentle and historically rooted way to pray through the week, aligning each day with one of God's ministering spirits. These blessings draw from scripture, Christian tradition, and the themes long associated with each archangel in German devotional life. Use them as you feel led—in the morning, at midday, or before rest.

This cycle requires no ritual items,
no specific gestures, no special learning.
Only a sincere heart, a quiet moment,
and a willingness to let God meet you where you are.

HOW TO USE THE ANGELIC WEEK

A simple guide for daily practice

You may use this cycle in any of the following ways:

- Read the blessing aloud each morning.
- Pray the associated Psalm during a quiet moment.
- Place the day's color somewhere in your room or on your desk.
- Write the day's name or theme on a small paper and keep it with you.
- Combine this practice with the canonical hours in Appendix B.

There is no formula, no strict rule, no requirement of perfection.
Only the gentle rhythm of petition, prayer, and trust.

SUNDAY — THE DAY OF MICHAEL

Theme: Courage, protection, truth
Color (historical): White or gold
Scripture: Psalm 27

Michael, the defender of God's people, has long stood as the guardian of courage and the shield against fear. On Sunday, Christians asked God to strengthen their hearts and guard them as they began a new week.

Blessing for Sunday:
"Lord God, give me the courage to walk in truth.
Let Your strength be my strength, and Your light my protection.
May the ministry of Michael keep fear from my mind
and guide me in all things that honor You. Amen."

MONDAY — THE DAY OF GABRIEL

Theme: Messages, clarity, guidance
Color: Blue or silver
Scripture: Luke 1:26–38

Gabriel brought messages of hope—first to Daniel, then to Mary herself. In German devotion, Monday became a day for seeking clarity, direction, and peace in decision-making.

Blessing for Monday:
"O God who sends Your messengers,
grant me clarity of thought and purity of intention.
As Gabriel brought good news,
let Your wisdom guide my steps today. Amen."

TUESDAY — THE DAY OF CAMAEL (KAMAUEL)

Theme: Strength, steadfastness, endurance
Color: Red
Scripture: Psalm 18

Camael, whose name means "one who sees God," appears in Christian tradition as an angel of perseverance and holy resolve. On Tuesdays, many Christians prayed for strength of will to endure hardship and finish their work with integrity.

Blessing for Tuesday:
"Lord of hosts, grant me steadfastness.
Strengthen my hands for the tasks before me
and steady my mind when I feel overwhelmed.
May the ministry of Camael give me endurance and peace. Amen."

WEDNESDAY — THE DAY OF RAPHAEL

Theme: Healing, travel, comfort
Color: Green
Scripture: Psalm 121

Raphael's name means "God heals." In the Book of Tobit—as preserved in Christian tradition—he guides, protects, and brings restoration. Wednesday became the day to pray for health of body, mind, and home.

Blessing for Wednesday:
"Heavenly Father, shelter me in Your mercy.
Comfort my spirit and bring healing to the wounded places within me.
As Raphael watched over travelers,
watch over my steps this day. Amen."

THURSDAY — THE DAY OF SACHIEL / ZADKIEL

Theme: Mercy, livelihood, blessing
Color: Purple or deep blue
Scripture: Psalm 112

Sachiel (often identified with Zadkiel in Christian tradition) is connected with generosity, blessing, and God's provision. Thursday has long been a day to ask for livelihood, financial peace, and mercy in all dealings.

Blessing for Thursday:
"Lord of mercy, bless the work of my hands.
Grant me integrity in my labor
and generosity in my heart.
Let Your provision sustain me,
and let Your mercy shape all my dealings today. Amen."

FRIDAY — THE DAY OF ANAEL / HANIEL

Theme: Peace, the home, relationships
Color: Rose or soft green
Scripture: Psalm 133

As the week's labors near their end, Friday invites prayers for harmony within the household and peace in every relationship. Anael (or Haniel) embodies gentleness, love, and reconciliation.

Blessing for Friday:
"God of peace, quiet my heart.
Guide my words and soften my spirit.
Bless my home, my loved ones, and all who cross my path.
May Your peace reign in every room. Amen."

SATURDAY — THE DAY OF CASSIEL

Theme: Boundaries, endings, spiritual rest
Color: Black or gray
Scripture: Psalm 23

Saturday has long been a day of closing the week, setting boundaries, returning burdens to God, and preparing for the Sabbath. Cassiel represents holy rest and the peace of letting go.

Blessing for Saturday:
"Good Shepherd, lead me into rest.
Help me release the worries of the week
and place them into Your hands.
Let Your peace settle upon my mind
and guard my sleep this night. Amen."

THE CHRISTIAN HOURS OF THE DAY
A Devotional "Prayer Clock" for Daily Life

Long before clocks governed the rhythm of our days, Christians marked time by prayer. These "canonical hours" formed the heartbeat of monastic life, but they also shaped the daily devotions of ordinary believers—farmers, craftsmen, homemakers, and rural families across Europe, including the Pennsylvania Germans who preserved so many of these traditions.

The hours are not magical moments or power windows; they are simply **invitations**.
They remind us that every rhythm of the day—from rising to working to resting—can become a moment to return to God.

In your own home, you may use these hours in whatever way fits your life.
You are not expected to keep the exact schedule of monks.
Instead, let these prayers breathe gently through your day, anchoring your heart in peace.

Each hour below includes:

- a traditional theme,
- a scripture,
- and a short blessing written for modern readers.

Use them freely.
Combine them with the angelic days if you wish.
Let them speak to you as you move through the hours God gives.

HOW TO USE THE PRAYER CLOCK

You may choose any of the following approaches:

A Single Hour Per Day

Perhaps Vespers in the evening, or Lauds at dawn.

"Touchpoints" — 2 or 3 hours

Dawn, midday, and night.
A gentle rhythm for busy lives.

Full Devotion (all hours, loosely kept)

Not by the clock—
but by the heart's memory.

Combined with the Angelic Week

For example:

- Sunday + Lauds = Courage & Blessing
- Friday + Vespers = Peace & Home Harmony

As a Blessing Cycle for the Household

Speak each hour's prayer in a different room of the home throughout the week.

There is no right way—only sincere intention.
Let these hours become anchors of grace in the turning of your day.

MATINS
(After Midnight)

Theme: Protection in darkness
Scripture: Psalm 91

In old households, Matins was prayed when someone woke in the night—an act of trust rather than fear. Night is not an enemy; it is a place where God watches while we cannot.

Blessing for Matins:
"Lord of the night, keep watch over me.
Calm my fears, guard my rest,
and let Your presence be the light that never fades. Amen."

PRIME
(First Hour of Day — roughly early morning)

Theme: Blessing of work
Scripture: Psalm 90:17

Prime sanctified the first task of the day. Whether work was in the field, workshop, schoolroom, or kitchen, Christians prayed that their labor would be honorable and fruitful.

Blessing for Prime:
"Lord, bless the work of my hands today.
Grant me diligence, clarity, and patience
in all I must do. Amen."

LAUDS
(Dawn)

Theme: Blessing the household
Scripture: Psalm 63

As light returned, families prayed for their homes, their work, and their loved ones. Dawn was a reminder that mercy renews each morning.

Blessing for Lauds:
"Father of lights, bless this home as the day begins.
Let peace rest in every room
and guide our steps in truth and gentleness. Amen."

TERCE
(Midmorning)

Theme: Peace of mind
Scripture: Philippians 4:6–7

Terce was the hour of settling one's spirit. The day's demands began to weigh on the mind, and believers prayed for calm hearts and wise thoughts.

Blessing for Terce:
"God of peace, steady my thoughts.
Quiet the worries that rise within me
and fill my mind with Your calm. Amen."

SEXT
(Midday)

Theme: Relief from fatigue
Scripture: Psalm 23

At noon, the weight of the day's labor became evident. Sext invited believers to pause, breathe, and ask God to refresh body and spirit.

Blessing for Sext:
"Shepherd of my soul, renew my strength.
Give rest to my weariness
and refresh me with Your presence.
Amen."

VESPERS
(Evening)

Theme: Protection for the home
Scripture: Psalm 121

As daylight faded, families gathered to pray for safety during the night. Vespers was a moment of gratitude and trust.

Blessing for Vespers:
"Guardian of Israel, watch over this home.
Let no harm draw near,
and let Your peace settle upon us as we rest. Amen."

NONE
(Afternoon / Ninth Hour)

Theme: Strength in adversity
Scripture: Psalm 46

None was prayed when the day's difficulties reached their height. It acknowledged human struggle without shame and asked God for courage, grace, and endurance.

Blessing for None:
"Lord, be my refuge in the midst of trial.
Give me strength to endure,
wisdom to act rightly,
and courage to finish this day with faith. Amen."

COMPLINE
(Night)

Theme: Rest and guarding dreams
Scripture: Psalm 4

Compline closed the day. It was the prayer of release—the quiet surrender of all worries, failures, and unfinished tasks into God's hands.

Blessing for Compline:
"Lord, into Your hands I place this day.
Grant me peaceful sleep and guard my dreams.
Let Your mercy cover all that remains undone. Amen."

Analog Traditions Across the World (For Study, Not Syncretism)

Christian / Germanic Practice	Jewish Tradition	Catholic / Orthodox Tradition	Islamic Tradition	West African / Afro-Diasporic Traditions	Indigenous Traditions	Persian (Pre-Islamic & Folk)	Wiccan / Pagan / Neo-Pagan	Far East Asian (Chinese, Korean)	Indian (Hindu & Folk)
Bible-Lot Casting (Psalms)	*Goral,* opening Psalms for comfort	*Sortes Sanctorum;* opening Psalter	Opening Qur'an for guidance (*fal al-Qur'an*)	Opening Ifá *odu* (reflective, not divinatory analogy)	Seeking signs through stories or land	*Arda Viraf* visionary guidance; casting sacred lots	Drawing runes or ogham blocks, *bibliomancy* (reflective practice)	*Jiaobei* (moon blocks), *bibliomancy* via Confucian texts	Opening Gita or Ramayana passages for comfort
Psalm Cycles (3/7/9 days)	Tehillim cycles	Novenas, Akathists	Dhikr repetitions	Multi-day ancestor rites	Multi-day spirit festivals	*Pateprayers* of expiation	Sabbat or esbat multi-day spiritual work	3-, 7-, 9-day devotional cycles in Buddhist & Taoist folk practice	Multi-day pujas, *vratas* (fasting/prayer cycles)
Boundary Walking	Blessing fields, mezuzah on doorposts	Processions & home blessings	Ayat al-Kursi recited over property	Water/earth perimeter rites	Land acknowledgment & medicine walks	Fire-circle purification rites	Casting protective circles (symbolic boundary)	Confucian/Taoist space-cleansing rituals	*Vastu* perimeter blessings

Cross-Marking Doors & Windows	Chalk inscriptions, protective verses	Epiphany chalking (CMB)	Qur'anic plaques at doorways	Veves at thresholds	Sacred icons above doors	Zoroastrian *kusti* knots near doors	Pentagrams or Brigid's cross	Fu talismans; Chinese door gods	Kolam/mandala threshold markings
Peace Strings / Prayer Cords	Tzitzit / fringes	Prayer ropes, rosaries	Misbaha beads	Beaded ancestor cords	Protective cords / yarn charms	*Kusti* cord tied with prayers	Knot magic; pagan prayer cords	Buddhist/Korean string talismans	Raksha threads, mala prayers
Alms-as-Remedy	*Tzedakah*	Works of mercy	*Sadaqah*	Offerings to ancestors	Gift-giving for harmony	Charity for soul purification	Offerings to gods/spirits	Almsgiving for karma balancing	
Herbal Household Blessings	Bitter herbs; balm	Holy herbs (Assumption)	Scented herbs	Plant offerings to ancestors	Smudging or herb offerings	Zoroastrian fragrant herbs	Herbal charms & pagan bundles	Burning mugwort; incense/herbs	Tulsi, neem, turmeric symbolic use
Paper Amulets (Zettel)	Psalms on parchment	Holy cards, icons	Ayat on cards	Ancestor papers	Story-symbol amulets	*Talismanic Pahlavi scripts*	Pagan sigils / witch bottles	Taoist fu talismans	Yantras, kavachas (paper/metal scripture)

Note: Although the chart above shows parallels across many world traditions, it is important to understand what these similarities truly mean. They reveal shared human instincts, not shared theology. Nearly every culture blesses doorways, marks thresholds, prays in cycles, carries sacred words, ties cords or knots as reminders, uses herbs symbolically, and places protective inscriptions in the home. These practices are not interchangeable or equal in meaning—they simply show that human beings everywhere seek God, the sacred, or the good through familiar devotional forms. The Christian German folk practices in this book remain distinct, grounded in scripture, prayer, and the gentle rhythms of Braucherei. Nothing in these comparisons is meant to encourage the blending of traditions; the parallels are offered only to honor the dignity of other cultures and to situate Hohman's world within a broader landscape of human devotion. Universal structures often arise without contact, which is why so many traditions independently developed ways to bless the home, walk boundaries, or carry small scripture tokens. The inclusion of Persian, Asian, Pagan, and other global traditions is therefore scholarly, not syncretic. Their presence shows that rural Christian households participated in a wider human pattern without undermining their uniqueness. These correspondences also help explain why later publishers misapplied the term "powwow" to this tradition: when surface similarities exist, people sometimes assume borrowing or mixture where none occurred. This edition restores clarity by acknowledging the parallels while firmly honoring the separate origins of each practice.

The Role of the Psalms as Universal Devotional Poetry

Across the Abrahamic world—Jewish, Christian, and Islamic—sacred texts have long served as balm for grief, protection in danger, a means of emotional steadiness, and a foundation for communal identity. The Psalms in particular occupy a place of extraordinary centrality. They are prayers of fear, thanksgiving, anger, hope, despair, and praise—all preserved in the very language of the human heart. For centuries, Christians in the German-speaking world turned to the Psalms not as spells or formulas but as familiar companions, believing that these ancient words could steady the mind and strengthen the spirit. In this way, the Psalms became a form of "medicine for the soul," offering comfort in suffering and clarity in confusion. Including a short sidebar titled **"Why the Psalms Were Considered Medicine for the Soul"** would help readers understand why Hohman and his neighbors relied so deeply on this book above all others.

The Role of Sound: Spoken Blessing as Healing

Throughout history, many cultures have believed that healing begins with the spoken word. Blessings, when spoken aloud, take on a rhythm and presence that written words alone do not carry. In Christian German Braucherei, the power of the spoken word was never magical; it was devotional. Practitioners used the Lord's Prayer, the Psalms, short scriptural verses, and simple repeated blessings to quiet fear, soothe pain, or ask God for protection. Speaking these prayers aloud allowed believers to participate actively in their faith, to hear truth in their own voice, and to speak God's promises into the moment of need. A short reflection titled **"Why Braucherei Emphasizes the Spoken Word"** would enrich the reader's understanding of this deeply embodied form of prayer.

Household Objects as Sacred Reminders

For many Christian German families, the home itself was a small sanctuary—
a place where the sacred met the ordinary. Simple objects such
as **Zettel** (paper amulets with scripture), **Breverl** (prayer packets),
and **Schutzbrief** (protection letters) were not charms or talismans but
reminders of God's nearness. They were placed above doorways, tucked into
Bibles, or carried in pockets as quiet affirmations of faith. These objects did
not contain power; rather, they pointed the heart toward God's power.
Similar practices exist in countless cultures worldwide, showing that human
beings instinctively sanctify their living spaces with words, symbols, and
gestures of devotion. A short section titled **"The Christian Home as a Place
of Daily Liturgy"** could beautifully frame this understanding.

Ethical Framework for Folk Practices

Any devotional tradition must rest upon an ethical foundation, and
Braucherei is no exception. The heart of Christian folk practice has always
been faithfulness to Christ's teachings: no coercion, no manipulation, no
superstition, no attempts to control others, and no belief that human beings
can compel divine action. These practices are not engines of power but
expressions of trust, humility, and care. By emphasizing that blessings must
never be used to dominate, deceive, or harm, you root this tradition firmly in
Christian ethics and distinguish it clearly from occult or coercive systems. A
concise reflection on this ethical posture would offer clarity and safeguard
readers from misunderstanding.

The Role of Community in Christian Folk Practice

Braucherei was never a solitary art. It lived in families, churches, farms, and neighborhoods. Mothers prayed healing over their children. Farmers prayed together over livestock during difficult seasons. Neighbors comforted the sick by reciting Psalms at their bedside. Families walked the land together, prayed over harvests, and supported one another in times of grief and danger. These practices were woven into the fabric of daily communal life. Including a section called **"Communal Aspects of Christian Folk Practice"** would help readers see that this tradition is fundamentally relational—rooted in love of neighbor, shared burdens, and mutual care.

The Role of Memory & Lineage

Christian folk practices did not arrive through formal instruction or institutional training—they were passed quietly from one generation to the next. A mother might teach her child which Psalm to speak during storms. A father might demonstrate how to pray before beginning a day's work. A neighbor might show a young family how to bless a home or soothe a troubled heart. Pastors, when approached, often affirmed these practices when they aligned with scripture and Christian virtue. This gentle transmission created a lineage of blessing, a living chain stretching across time. A short reflection titled **"The Living Lineage of Blessing"** would offer readers a sense of belonging to a heritage of ordinary people seeking God through simple acts of faith.

HERBS & HOUSEHOLD BLESSINGS
Symbolic, Devotional Uses of the Gifts of the Earth

Herbs have always played a quiet role in the devotional life of Christian households. In rural German-speaking communities, plants were not treated as sources of magical power but as reminders of God's provision—visible signs of His care woven into the rhythms of daily life. Families dried herbs above the stove, bundled flowers to scent the home, or placed sprigs in Bibles, not for occult purposes, but as **symbols of comfort, gratitude, and peace**.

This appendix restores that gentle tradition in a way appropriate for the modern reader.
Nothing here is medicinal advice or instruction.
Nothing is meant to replace proper medical care.
Instead, these practices use herbs symbolically—as objects of reflection, reminders of scripture, and aids to prayer.

Each plant is presented with three things:

1. Its **historical devotional use** among German/Pennsylvania German Christians
2. Its **symbolic meaning** in this tradition
3. A **safe, modern, purely spiritual application** you may incorporate at home

Let these herbs become quiet companions to your prayer life, as they once were for countless households who lived close to the land and trusted God for every need.

HERBS COMMONLY USED IN PENNSYLVANIA GERMAN HOUSEHOLDS

CHAMOMILE
Symbol of Calmness & Rest

Historical Use:
Chamomile was dried in many Christian German households as a relaxing fragrance.
Mothers often kept small bundles near children's beds as a symbol of peace.

Symbolic Meaning:
Calmness, emotional rest, and the easing of worry.

Devotional Application:
Place a small bundle on a nightstand and pray:
"Lord, quiet my thoughts and grant me peaceful rest."

COMFREY
Symbol of Emotional Mending

Historical Use:
Comfrey roots and leaves were commonly grown, though their medicinal use is outdated today.
Symbolically, it represented *binding up wounds*.

Symbolic Meaning:
Healing of the heart and mending of broken places within the spirit.

Devotional Application:
Place a dried leaf in a Bible at Psalm 147 ("He heals the brokenhearted").
Let it be a reminder of God's restorative presence.

YARROW
Symbol of Courage & Steadfastness

Historical Use:
Yarrow grew along fields and pathways and was valued as a sign of resilience.

Symbolic Meaning:
Courage, bravery, endurance.

Devotional Application:
Carry a small dried sprig as a reminder when facing difficult tasks or decisions.

SAINT JOHN'S WORT
Symbol of Joy & Light

Historical Use:
Associated with the midsummer season in Christian Europe, used symbolically to represent Christ's light.

Symbolic Meaning:
Joy, uplifted spirit, victory over gloom.

Devotional Application:
Place a small yellow flower in a jar of water as a reminder to "walk in the light."

PLANTAIN
Symbol of Protection & Watchfulness

Historical Use:
Plantain was known as "the traveler's herb," growing along wagon paths and roads.

Symbolic Meaning:
Protection, safety during travel, and watchfulness.

Devotional Application:
Place a leaf (or a photo of one) near your front door as you pray Psalm 121.

THYME
Symbol of Strength & Courage

Historical Use:
Thyme bundles hung in kitchens as a fragrant reminder of strength and endurance.

Symbolic Meaning:
Boldness, perseverance, strength for the day's work.

Devotional Application:
Hold a leaf while praying for strength to complete a difficult task.

SAGE
Symbol of Clarity & Wisdom

(NOT used as smoke cleansing in this tradition — that practice belongs to other cultures.)

Historical Use:
Sage was a common kitchen herb symbolizing wisdom, not ritual smoke cleansing.

Symbolic Meaning:
Clarity, good sense, sober-mindedness.

Devotional Application:
Place a leaf on your desk or workspace while praying for discernment.

LEMON BALM
Symbol of Comfort & Consolation

Historical Use:
Used to brighten the home with fragrance.
Associated with comfort during sorrow.

Symbolic Meaning:
Soothing of grief, emotional comfort, reassurance.

Devotional Application:
Keep a small dried sprig beside Psalm 34 ("The Lord is close to the brokenhearted").

MINT
Symbol of Refreshment & Renewal

Historical Use:
Mint grew in nearly every German homestead garden.
Its aroma was associated with refreshment and welcome.

Symbolic Meaning:
Renewal, refreshment, hospitality.

Devotional Application:
Place a small sachet of mint in an entryway to remind your household to welcome others with grace.

CHICORY
Symbol of Steadfastness & Perseverance

Historical Use:
Chicory often grew stubbornly in roadside soil—seen as a picture of perseverance.

Symbolic Meaning:
Determination, resilience, quiet strength.

Devotional Application:
Use a chicory flower or drawing as a bookmark for Psalm 27.

HOREHOUND
Symbol of Endurance & Resolve

Historical Use:
Once grown for its hardy, bitter leaves; symbolically linked to endurance.

Symbolic Meaning:
Steadfastness in adversity.

Devotional Application:
Hold a leaf during prayer when facing trials.

VALERIAN
Symbol of Stillness & Rest

Historical Use:
Valerian's strong scent made it a symbol of deep rest in German households.

Symbolic Meaning:
Quietude, stillness, deep inner peace.

Devotional Application:
Place near your bed with the prayer: "Be still, my soul, and know that He is God."

ANGELICA ROOT
Symbol of Blessing & Divine Favor

Historical Use:
Angelica was associated with St. Michael's Day and often considered a plant of blessing.

Symbolic Meaning:
Blessing, divine favor, protection through prayer.

Devotional Application:
Place a small root near a family Bible as a symbol of God's blessing upon the household.

HOUSEHOLD APPLICATIONS (NON-MEDICAL, NON-INGESTIVE)

Here are safe, symbolic ways you may use herbs in devotional life today.

THE HEART OF THIS PRACTICE

These herbs do not hold power. They simply remind the heart of God's promises.

They help quiet the mind, focus intention, and evoke gratitude. They bridge creation and devotion, connecting daily life to daily prayer.

Blessing Bowls

Fill a small bowl with water and place herbs symbolically inside. The water is not for drinking—only for reflection.

Pray over the bowl:
"Lord, let Your peace abide in this home."

Peace Sachets

Place dried herbs in a small cloth pouch.
Carry it, keep it in a drawer, or place it by the bed as a symbolic reminder of peace.

Reflection Tea

You may brew any herbal tea safely purchased from a store—
but the act is symbolic, not prescriptive.
Drink while reading a Psalm.

Scripture-Blooms

Press a leaf or flower between the pages of your Bible near a passage that speaks to you.
Let it become a reminder of the prayer you prayed there.

Room Blessings (Symbolic Water)

Dip your fingers into a bowl of clean water and touch the doorframe.
Speak a short blessing:
"Peace to those who enter. Blessing to those who depart."

CLOSING BENEDICTION

Go forth in the peace of the Lord.
May His light guard your steps,
His truth steady your heart,
and His mercy surround your home.
May every room you dwell in be filled with calm,
every place you walk be held in safety,
and every burden you carry be lifted in His strength.
May your nights bring rest,
your mornings bring clarity,
and your days be crowned with quiet blessings.
And as you go, may the Lord bless thee and keep thee;
may His face shine upon thee and give thee peace,
now and always,
Amen.

AFTERWORD

As you close this volume, you join a long line of readers who have carried *The Long Lost Friend* through seasons of hardship, hope, change, and renewal. What began as a small book in a young nation became, across two centuries, a companion to immigrants, a comfort to rural families, a curiosity to scholars, and a quiet treasure to those who believed that the presence of God could be felt in daily life.

This updated edition stands not as a replacement for the original, but as a continuation of its purpose. The world that shaped Hohman has vanished, but the human spirit has not. We still worry. We still suffer. We still seek guidance. We still turn to scripture for wisdom, to prayer for help, and to simple acts of devotion for grounding in an unsteady age.

If the material in this book has brought you calm, clarity, or strength; if it has offered a word to steady your heart, a prayer to lift your breath, or a blessing for someone you love, then its purpose is fulfilled. The tradition lives on because you have taken it into your hands and into your life.

Carry these words with humility.
Speak them with kindness.
Share them only in peace.
And may the same God who watched over the homes, fields, and families of 1820 watch over yours in the years to come.

Go forward with courage,
knowing that the ancient hope remains:

"God is our refuge and strength."

Now and always.

Also Hear These Works in the Voice of Dennis Logan

Over the past decade I have devoted thousands of hours to recording sacred texts, apocrypha, and esoteric classics.

If **The Prodigal – Wow A Long Lost Friend Returns** deepened your understanding, you can continue the journey through our expanding library of works in scripture, apocrypha, esoterica, philosophy, folklore, mysticism, and political thought.

You will find many of the texts referenced in our Legitimate Sacred Texts Catalog, our Legitimate Esoteric & Occult Corpus, and even the works that inform our Grand Catalog of Hoaxes and Pseudepigrapha—all read, rendered, and reissued with care.

To explore the complete catalogue of 100+ **audiobooks**, from the Bible and Koran to grimoires, mystic treatises, revolutionary texts, and the great currents of world literature:

Search "Dennis Logan" on Audible.

New titles are released monthly as part of Penemue Media's ongoing commitment to clarity, preservation, and the restoration of our shared intellectual lineage.

Scripture, Apocrypha & Ancient Texts

- *The Universal Bible of the Protestant, Catholic, Orthodox, Ethiopic, Syriac, and Samaritan Church*
- *Lost Books of the Bible: The Great Rejected Texts*
- *The Book of Jasher*
- *Book of Enoch, Jubilees, Jasher & The Book of Giants: The Complete Scriptures of Nephilim & Fallen Angels*
- *The Books of Enoch and The Book of Giants (featuring 1, 2, and 3 Enoch with the Aramaic and Manichean Giants texts)*
- *The Book of Jubilees: The Little Genesis, The Apocalypse of Moses*
- *The First and Second Books of Adam and Eve*
- *The Pentautech: The 5 Books of Moses*
- *The War Scroll: The War of the Sons of Light Against the Sons of Darkness*
- *The Kebra Nagast : The Glory of the Kings*
- *The Book of the Bee: The Syriac Text*
- *The Holy Piby: The Blackman's Bible*
- *The Gospel of Nicodemus, the Acts of Pilate and the Harrowing of Hell*
- *The Books of Jasher*

Magick & Occult Classics

- *The Universal One: Walter Russell's Foundational Mind-Centered Electromagnetic Universe Treatise-Exact Facsimile with Full Illustrations*
- *Paradoxes of the Highest Science*
- *Aradia: The Gospel of the Witches*
- *The Magus or Celestial Intelligencer: A Modern Rendering of the 1801 Edition*
- *The Book of the Sacred Magic of Abramelin the Mage: A Modern Rendering of the 15th Century Grimoire*
- *The Lesser Key of Solomon: A Modern Rendering of the 17th Century Grimoire*
- *The Greater Key of Solomon: A Modern Rendering of the 15th Century Grimoire*
- *An Outline of Occult Science: A Modern Edition*
- *A Textbook of Theosophy*

Gnostic, Mystical & Esoteric Studies

- *Banned from the Bible*
- *The Secret Gospel of Mark*
- *The Gospel of Barnabas*
- *The Gospel of Judas: The Man, His History, His Story*
- *The Aquarian Gospel of Jesus the Christ*
- *The Gnostic Gospels of Philip, Mary Magdalene, and Thomas*
- *The Gnostic Scriptures*
- *An Advanced Lesson in Gnosticism*
- *The Apocryphon of John: A Gnostic Gospel*
- *The Secret Teachings of All Ages*
- *The Kybalion, Tablet of Hermes & Emerald Tablets*
- *Thought-Forms*
- *The Initiates of the Flame*
- *Golden Verses of Pythagoras & Other Pythagorean Fragments*
- *Science of Breath*
- *The Way of Initiation: How to Attain Knowledge of the Higher Worlds: A Modern Edition*
- *The Education of Children: From the Standpoint of Theosophy: A Modern Edition*

Original Works by Dennis Logan

- *The Panerotic Sutras of Master Stryfe*
- *The Apocatastasis of Enoch*
- *The Testament of Samson*
- *Try Satan: How One Man Outwitted the Devil, Misplaced His Wife, & Broke the Wheels of Fate*